THE *Guilty Pleasures* COOKBOOK

DEVELOPING A DELICIOUS AND DISCIPLINED RELATIONSHIP WITH GUILTY PLEASURE FOODS ONE RECIPE AT A TIME

Vincent Tropepe

MAIN ENTREE PUBLISHING

Copyright (c) 2025 by Vincent A. Tropepe
All rights reserved
Published in the United States of America
Library of Congress Cataloging - in - Publication Data
Tropepe, Vincent A - 1st ed.
The Guilty Pleasure Cookbook: Developing a Delicious and Disciplined Relationship
With Guilty Pleasure Foods, One Recipe at A Time

I. Recipes
II. Multiple Cuisines
III. Cooking

Printed in the United States of America
Photography by Vincent A. Tropepe
10 9 8 7 6 5 4 3 2 1

First Edition

Other Books By Chef Tropepe

IN MY WHITES

A Matter of Culinary Perspective (2016)

SLAUGHTERED

How Inconsistent Lockdowns Collapsed The Hospitality Industry During COVID-19 (2021)

ROASTED, CHOPPED & BEATEN

When Cities Declare War On The Restaurants That Feed Them (2022)

ROOTS

Unlocking The Potential & Discovering The Delicious In All Natural Ingredients (2023)

THE OTHER FIVE SENSES

Understanding The Art of Hospitality (2024)

Dedication...

This book is dedicated to the many people who have continued to offer me encouragement, love and concern. You make the world a better place.

Todd Babcock
Michael Babcock
Salvatore Baretta
Daymein Christopher
Joseph DiVittorio
Ken Doughtery
Aaron Forman
Salvatore Forte
Jayden Martin
Richard Montalbano
David Rivera
Glen Rolnick

In Loving Memory Of...

Loved, constantly missed & always remembered

MaryAnn Fitzgerald
Daniele Kucera
Rick Sommers Steinhaus

A Note From Chef Tropepe

For far too long, society at large, as well as the people around us, has demonized certain foods, often labeling them as "guilty pleasures." Our relationship with the food we consume is not only a personal choice but also a reflection of our identity and upbringing. However, no one should feel shame for who they are or for the cultural and personal influences that shape them.

In my mid-to-late 20s, I was significantly larger than I am now. At the time, I had a 52-inch waist and weighed approximately 420 pounds. I made a conscious decision to lose the weight, but in order to do so, I first needed to identify the root of the problem. I had to sit down with myself and ask, How did I get to this size? This self-reflection required honesty, objectivity, and self-compassion. Ultimately, I discovered two key factors contributing to my weight gain: (1) I used food as an emotional coping mechanism, and (2) as a line cook in an expensive restaurant, I worked 12- to 14-hour shifts without structured meals. By the time I finished work—often at 1 or 2 a.m.—I would grab fast food on my way home, eat quickly, and go straight to sleep, only to wake up a few hours later and repeat the cycle. This pattern of eating and sleeping was a major factor in my weight gain.

Once I identified the underlying issues, I needed a clear plan. Initially, I tried to cut out all foods I considered "bad," but I quickly realized this approach was unsustainable. Whenever I reintroduced those foods, I would overindulge—eating not just one Boston Cream doughnut, but four. This all-or-nothing mindset was counterproductive.

Through discipline, exercise, portion control, and mindful eating, I eventually lost weight naturally, reaching 220 pounds with a 32-inch waist. However, I soon realized that my tendency to overeat treats stemmed from complete deprivation. This approach was flawed. Moderation, not elimination, is key to developing a healthy, sustainable relationship with food.

Occasionally indulging in "guilty pleasure" foods plays an important role in our emotional well-being, a fact supported by scientific research. Many people, including myself, initially believe that cutting out certain foods entirely is the most effective way to lose weight. However, my experience taught me that fostering a balanced relationship with food leads to long-term success far more than strict avoidance.

When I set out to write this book, my goal was clear: to provide a guide that helps people build a balanced relationship with the food they love. It is time to move away from the demonization of certain foods and ingredients.

Guilty pleasure foods are not going to disappear; they are an integral part of cultures around the world. Instead of avoiding them, we should celebrate them. We should prepare and share them with friends and family in a way that is healthy, moderate, and balanced. After all, food is one of the fundamental ways we connect with one another as human beings.

xxxx

Table Of Contents

CHAPTER ONE SAVORY

Mac 'n Cheese	20
Chicken and Waffles	22
Lasagna	25
Chili Cheese Fries	26
Double Pork Double Beef Cheeseburger	28
Bacon, Lettuce and Tomato Sandwich	30
Homemade Potato Chips	32
Homemade Pizza	35
Mashed Potato	37
Baked Beans	39
Corn Dogs	40
Southern Style Biscuits	42
Chicken Fried Steak with Gravy	44
Steak au Poivre	46
Chicken Parmesan	48
Baked Ziti	50
Classic Grilled Cheese	53
New England Clam Chowder	54
Chicken Wings	56
Oven Baked Nachos	57
Fish and Chips	62
Chicken Nuggets	64
Cheese Perogies with Bacon and Onions	65
Chili	67
Drunken Meatloaf	68
Roasted Chicken	69

CHAPTER TWO SWEET

Classic Vanilla Cupcakes	74
New York Style Cheesecake	76
Brownies	78
Boston Cream Pie	79
S'Mores	82
Chocolate Mousse	83
Bread Pudding with Caramel Bourbon Sauce	84
Challah French Toast	86
Buttermilk Pancakes	88
Cinnamon Rolls	89
Churros with Chocolate Sauce	91
Chocolate Chip Cookies	93
Pistachio Layer Cake	96
Dutch Apple Pie	99
Lemon Bars	101
Coconut Layer Cake	103
All Butter Pound Cake	106
Banana Cream Pie	107
Italian Cream Puffs with Cannoli Cream	110
Creme Brulee	112
Tarte Tatin	113
Lemon Meringue Pie	114
Tiramisu	117
Peach Cobbler	119
Rice Pudding	120
Index	122

Chapter One
January

Mac 'n Cheese

Ingredients: **Yields: 8 servings**

1 lb.	Dried elbow or small shell pasta
$1/2$ cup.	Unsalted butter
$1/2$ cup.	All Purpose flour
$1^{1/2}$ cups.	Whole milk
$2^{1/2}$ cups.	Half and Half
4 cups.	Cheddar cheese, shredded
2 cups.	Gruyere cheese, shredded
$1/2$ Tbsp.	Salt
$1/2$ tsp.	Black pepper
$1/4$ tsp.	Paprika

Instructions:

Preheat the oven to 325 degrees F and grease a 3-qt baking dish (9x13"). Set aside.

Bring a large pot of salted water to a boil. When boiling, add dried pasta and cook 1 minute less than the package directs for al dente. Drain and drizzle with a little olive oil to keep from sticking.

While water is coming up to a boil, shred cheeses and toss together to mix, then divide into three piles. Approximately 3 cups for the sauce, $1^{1/2}$ cups for the inner layer, and $1^{1/2}$ cups for the topping.

Melt butter in a large saucepan over medium heat. Sprinkle in flour and whisk to combine. Mixture will look like very wet sand. Cook for approximately 1 minute, whisking often. Slowly pour in about 2 cups or so of the half and half, while whisking constantly, until smooth. Slowly pour in the remaining half and half plus the whole milk, while whisking constantly, until combined and smooth.

Continue to heat over medium heat, whisking very often, until thickened to a very thick consistency. It should almost be the consistency of a semi-thinned-out condensed soup.

Remove from the heat and stir in spices and $1^{1/2}$ cups of the cheeses, stirring to melt and combine. Stir in another $1^{1/2}$ cups of cheese, and stir until completely melted and smooth.

In a large mixing bowl, combine the drained pasta with the cheese sauce, stirring to combine fully. Pour half of the pasta mixture into the prepared baking dish. Top with $1^{1/2}$ cups of shredded cheeses, then top that with the remaining pasta mixture.

Sprinkle the top with the last $1^{1/2}$ cups of cheese and bake for 15 minutes, until cheese is bubbly and lightly golden brown.

Chicken and Waffles

Ingredients:

Yields: 8 servings

8	Boneless, skinless chicken thighs
As needed	Vegetable Oil, for Deep frying

Ingredients for Buttermilk Brine:

2 cups.	Buttermilk
1 Tbsp.	Kosher salt
½ Tbsp.	Garlic powder
½ Tbsp.	Onion powder
1 Tbsp.	Hot sauce or Chili powder
1 tsp.	Smoked Paprika

Ingredients for Seasoned Flour Crust:

3 cups.	All Purpose flour
⅓ cup.	Cornstarch
2 tsp.	Baking powder
2 tsp.	Garlic powder
2 tsp.	Onion powder
2 tsp.	Kosher salt
2 tsp.	Black pepper

Ingredients for Spicy Honey Butter Sauce:

¼ cup.	Honey
½ tsp.	Chili powder
4 Tbsp.	Unsalted butter, softened and room temperature
½ tsp.	Kosher salt

Ingredients for Belgium Waffles:

2 ¼ cups.	All Purpose flour
1 Tbsp.	Baking powder
¼ cup.	Granulated sugar
½ tsp.	Kosher salt
1 tsp.	Cinnamon, ground
2	Eggs, large and separated
½ cup.	Vegetable Oil
2 cups.	Whole Milk
2 tsp.	Vanilla Extract

Instructions for Brine:

Whisk the buttermilk, Kosher salt, garlic powder, onion powder, hot sauce, and smoked paprika together in a large mixing bowl.

Add the boneless, skinless chicken thighs to the bowl, making sure every thigh is covered in the brine. Cover the bowl with plastic wrap and let the chicken marinate in the buttermilk brine from 1 hour to overnight in the refrigerator.

Instructions for Chicken:

In a dutch oven pot, heat up about half the pot's worth of vegetable oil. Allow the oil to reach 350 degrees F (180 degrees C/ 160 degrees C if using a fan-forced oven).

While the oil is heating up, in a mixing bowl whisk together flour, cornstarch, baking powder, and seasonings. Take each chicken thigh from the brine and dredge into the seasoned flour. Thoroughly coat the chicken all over, then let rest on a plate for five minutes before frying.

Fry the chicken in the hot oil (no more than about 4 thighs per batch) until golden brown, crispy, and cooked through completely, about 8-9 minutes.

Carefully take the chicken out of the oil and place them on a baking sheet fitted with a wire rack and let cool slightly before serving. Repeat until all the chicken thighs are fried.

Instructions for Spicy Honey Butter Sauce:

In a small saucepan, melt butter over medium heat with honey, Chili Powder, and Kosher Salt. Whisk well until the mixture is incorporated and homogenized.

Instructions for Waffles:

Begin to preheat your Belgian waffle iron, spray with non stick cooking spray.

In a large bowl, whisk together flour, baking powder, sugar, salt, and cinnamon.

In a separate medium sized bowl or stand mixer, beat the egg whites with a hand mixer until stiff peaks form, do not go further once they make stiff peaks or they'll break. Set aside.

In a large measuring cup (or another medium sized bowl) whisk together the egg yolks, vegetable oil, milk, and vanilla extract.

Whisk the wet mixture into the dry ingredients and mix until most of the lumps are gone, then gently fold in the egg whites with a rubber spatula.

Pour the batter into your ready preheated waffle iron and cook according to the waffle iron's directions.

Lasagna

Ingredients: **Yields: 4 servings**

1 lb.	Italian Sausage, sweet	1 ½ tsp.	Salt
¾ lb.	Ground Beef, lean	1 tsp.	Italian seasoning
½ cup.	White Onion, minced	½ tsp.	Fennel seeds
2 cloves.	Garlic, crushed	¼ tsp.	Black pepper
28 oz.	Canned tomatoes, crushed	12	Lasagna noodles
13 oz.	Tomato sauce	1 lb.	Ricotta cheese, whole milk
12 oz.	Tomato paste	1	Egg, large
½ cup.	Water	¾ lb.	Mozzarella cheese, sliced
2 Tbsp.	Granulated sugar	¾ cup	Parmesan cheese, grated
4 Tbsp.	Parsley, chopped fine		
1 ½ tsp.	Dried basil leaves		

Instructions:

Cook sausage, ground beef, onion, and garlic in a Dutch Oven over medium heat until well browned.

Stir in crushed tomatoes, tomato sauce, tomato paste, and water. Season with sugar, 2 tablespoons parsley, basil, 1 teaspoon salt, Italian seasoning, fennel seeds, and Black pepper. Simmer, covered, for about 1 ½ hours, stirring occasionally.

Bring a large pot of lightly salted water to a boil. Cook lasagna noodles in boiling water for 8 to 10 minutes. Drain noodles, and rinse with cold water.

In a mixing bowl, combine ricotta cheese with egg, remaining 2 tablespoons parsley, and $1/2$ teaspoon salt.

Preheat the oven to 375 degrees F (190 degrees C).

To assemble, spread 1 ½ cups of meat sauce in the bottom of a 9x13-inch baking dish. Arrange 6 noodles lengthwise over meat sauce, overlapping slightly. Spread with $1/2$ of the ricotta cheese mixture. Top with $1/3$ of the mozzarella cheese slices. Spoon 1 ½ cups meat sauce over mozzarella, and sprinkle with $1/4$ cup Parmesan cheese.

Repeat layers, and top with remaining mozzarella and Parmesan cheese. Cover with foil: to prevent sticking, either spray foil with cooking spray or make sure the foil does not touch the cheese.

Bake in the preheated oven for 25 minutes. Remove the foil and bake for an additional 25 minutes.

Rest lasagna for 15 minutes before serving.

Chili Cheese Fries

Yields: 8 servings

Ingredients for Chili:

1 tsp.	Vegetable oil	1 tsp.	Smoked Paprika
1 lb.	Ground beef (90% lean)	1 tsp.	Cocoa powder
1/2 cup.	White onion finely diced	1/2 tsp	Brown sugar
1 tsp.	Garlic, minced	1 tsp	Salt
15 oz.	Tomatoes, diced do not drain	1/4 tsp.	Black pepper
8 oz.	Tomato sauce	15 oz.	Kidney beans, drained and rinsed
1/2 cup	Beef broth		
1 Tbsp.	Chili powder		
1 tsp.	Cumin, ground		

Ingredients for fries:

32 oz.	French Fries, fresh or frozen
2 cups.	Cheddar cheese, shredded
As needed.	Assorted toppings as desired
As needed.	Cooking spray

Instructions for Chili:

Heat the oil in a large pot over medium high heat. Add the ground beef and season with 3/4 teaspoon salt and 1/4 teaspoon Black pepper. Cook, breaking up the meat with a spoon, for 3-4 minutes. Drain off any excess grease.

Add the onion to the pot and cook for an additional 3-4 minutes or until softened. Stir in the garlic and cook for 30 seconds.

Add the diced tomatoes, tomato sauce, beef broth, chili powder, ground cumin, smoked paprika, cocoa powder, brown sugar and 1/4 teaspoon salt to the pot. Bring to a simmer.

Cook for 30-40 minutes, stirring occasionally, or until chili has thickened.

Add the kidney beans and cook for another 10 minutes.

Taste and add more salt and pepper if desired.

Instructions for Fries:

Coat a sheet pan with cooking spray.

Cook the French Fries in the oven in a single layer on a sheet pan according to package directions.

Remove the pan of fries from the oven. Turn the oven heat to 400 degrees F.

You can finish the fries on a sheet pan, or transfer them to a skillet for a restaurant style presentation.

Spoon $1^{1/2}$ cups of chili over the fries, then top with cheddar cheese.

Return the fries to the oven. Bake for 5 minutes or until cheese is melted.

Add toppings if desired, then serve immediately.

How Chili Cheese Fries Became Famous

Chili cheese fries became popular because they combine three universally loved comfort foods into one dish (1) crispy fries; (2) savory chili and (3) melted cheese. This rich, flavorful combination appeals to a wide audience and satisfies multiple cravings at one time. Their rise in popularity can be traced to the mid-20th century American diners and drive-ins, where hearty, affordable meals were in high demand. These eateries helped turn chili cheese fries into a classic side dish or even a meal in itself, especially in regions like Southwest where chili has strong culinary roots.

The dish also gained traction thanks to its appeal as a social and shareable food, making it a favorite at bars, sports venues and fast food chains. As American food culture increasingly embraced bold, over-the-top flavors, chili cheese fries fit right in with the trend of piling on ingredients for maximum taste and satisfaction. Regional chains and national franchises further popularized the dish by including it on their menus, spreading it far beyond its regional origins.

Double Pork Double Beef Cheeseburger

Ingredients: **Yields: 2 servings**

2 1/2 lbs.	Beef chuck, ground (80% lean ground beef)
1 tsp.	Black pepper, ground
1 tsp.	Garlic powder
1 tsp.	Onion powder
1 tsp.	Ground mustard
2 tsp.	Worcestershire sauce
1 Tbsp.	Vegetable oil, for cooking
1 1/2 tsp.	Kosher salt
8 slices.	Cheddar cheese
2	Hamburger buns (lightly toasted, if desired)
8	Bacon sliced, cooked and crispy
8	Black Pepper Ham slices, thin

Instructions:

In a large bowl, combine the beef, pepper, garlic powder, onion powder, ground mustard, and Worcestershire sauce. (Do not put the salt in the mixture; you'll add it later.) Using your hands, mix until evenly combined. Form the meat into 4 large meatballs (about 4½ oz each), then pat each ball into a 1-inch-thick disc; smooth out the edges as best you can. Refrigerate for at least 15 minutes or until ready to cook (up to 24 hours, covered).

Turn on your exhaust fan and heat a 12-inch cast-iron or nonstick skillet over medium-high heat. Remove the patties from the fridge and season all over with the salt. Coat the hot pan evenly with the oil. Place the burgers on the skillet one at a time, firmly smashing them flat with a metal spatula until about ¼-inch thick before adding and smashing the next one. Let cook for about 2 minutes until nicely browned and crusty on the bottom. Flip the burgers and top with the cheese; cook for about 2 minutes more for medium-rare to medium burgers, or 3 minutes for medium to medium-well burgers.

Place the two burgers on the buns and top them with the bacon, black pepper ham and any other toppings you wish.

Tip:

Freezer-Friendly Instructions: The uncooked burgers can be frozen for up to three months. (Freeze the burgers on a baking sheet so their shape sets, then transfer them to a sealable plastic bag for easy storage.) Defrost the burgers overnight in the refrigerator prior to serving and then cook as directed.

Bacon, Lettuce and Tomato Sandwich

Ingredients: **Yields: 1 servings**

4	Bacon slices, cooked and crispy
2	Lettuce leaves
2	Tomato slices
2	Bread slices, toasted
1 Tbsp.	Mayonnaise

Instructions:

Cook bacon in a large, deep skillet over medium-high heat until evenly browned, about 10 minutes. Drain bacon on a paper towel-lined plate.

Arrange cooked bacon, lettuce, and tomato slices on one slice of bread. Spread mayonnaise on the other slice of bread.

Close to make a sandwich.

Fun Facts About The BLT Sandwich

1. The components of a Bacon, Lettuce & Tomato sandwich have been used in sandwiches as far back as 1900 and served in Victorian England.

2. The BLT sandwich gained much popularity after WWII thanks to grocery store refrigeration improvements. This made lettuce and tomatoes have a longer shelf life and available year round.

3. July is National BLT sandwich month in the United States.

4. In 2008 a 209 foot long BLT sandwich was made in Michigan setting a world record.

5. A BLT sandwich is truly all about balance. Saltiness of the bacon, juicy and sweet tomatoes, creaminess from the mayonnaise. To make an excellent BLT sandwich is an art.

Homemade Potato Chips

Ingredients: Yields: 8 servings

4	Russet potatoes, sliced paper thin
3 Tbsp.	Salt, plus more to taste
1 qt.	Vegetable Oil, for deep frying

Instructions:

Wash, dry and then thinly slice your potatoes using a mandolin.

Transfer potato slices to a large bowl of cold water as you slice them.

Drain slices and rinse under cold water. Refill the bowl with water, add 3 tablespoons salt, and put slices back in the bowl. Let potatoes soak in the salty water for at least 30 minutes.

Drain and rinse slices again. Pat dry.

Heat oil in a deep-fryer to 365 degrees F (185 degrees C).

Working in small batches, fry potato slices until golden.

Remove with a slotted spoon and drain on paper towels.

Continue until all of the slices are fried.

Season potato chips with additional salt if desired.

Some Chip History

Chef George Crum in 1853 created the potato chip at a restaurant called Moon's Lake House in Saratoga Springs, New York. Crum created the potato chip accidentally, as a customer in the dining room kept sending back his French fries complaining they were to thick. In a sarcastic move, Crum cut them so thin and fried them they became an instant hit not only with the picky customer, but with everyone.

In the 1920's Laura Scudder a California entrepreneur revolutionized the potato chip business by packaging the chips in wax paper bags sealing in freshness, it is with this that allowed the potato chip to get mass distribution into retail markets.

Pizza 101
An Education and Reflection

Having been born and raised in the Bensonhurst neighborhood of Brooklyn, New York, and as a full-blooded Italian, I certainly have an encyclopedia of knowledge on the subject of pizza. While many regions in the United States have developed their own styles—such as Detroit-style and Chicago deep-dish—nothing compares to a classic Brooklyn slice. However, pizza in America was not always the beloved cultural staple it is today. In the early 1900s, it was an inexpensive street food, made casalinga (home-style) by Southern Italian immigrant women in their kitchens. These women were the unsung pioneers who passed down the traditions that would eventually shape the American pizza landscape.

Adverse economic conditions forced four million Southern Italians to migrate to other countries by the early 1900s, bringing their culinary traditions with them. In 1905, Gennaro Lombardi applied for the first license to make and sell pizza in the United States at his grocery store on Spring Street, in what was then a thriving Italian-American neighborhood of New York City. His influence paved the way for others.

In 1912, Joe's Tomato Pie opened in Trenton, New Jersey. Twelve years later, Anthony (Totonno) Pero left Lombardi's to open Totonno's in Coney Island. In 1925, Frank Pepe founded his now-famous pizzeria in New Haven, Connecticut, and in 1929, John Sasso—another Lombardi's alum—established John's Pizza in Greenwich Village. The 1930s saw pizza spreading across the country, with Santarpio's opening in Boston in 1933 and Tommaso's arriving in San Francisco in 1934. That same year, Sciortino's opened in Perth Amboy, New Jersey. By the early 1940s, Chicago had birthed deep-dish pizza with the opening of Uno's. The common thread connecting these early pizzerias was their location in industrial cities where Italian immigrants worked in factories, helping introduce pizza to the broader American public.

The mainstreaming of pizza in American life accelerated after World War II. American GIs stationed in Italy returned home with a newfound appreciation for the pizza they had enjoyed overseas. In 1945, one of these returning soldiers, Ira Nevin, revolutionized the industry by developing the first gas-fired Baker's Pride pizza oven. This innovation allowed pizzerias to bake pizzas quickly, cleanly, efficiently, and cost-effectively.

Between 1945 and 1960, pizzerias sprouted up nationwide. Most were independently owned, primarily by Italian and Greek immigrants. These pizzerias prided themselves on using fresh ingredients—making their own dough, crafting sauces from fresh or canned Italian tomatoes, and sourcing mozzarella from local cheesemongers. Pizza quickly became a staple for workers on lunch breaks, families seeking an affordable yet satisfying meal, and late-night patrons looking for a post-drinking snack. The end of Prohibition in 1933 further fueled this trend, as many pizzerias doubled as taverns. The communal nature of pizza—traditionally served whole rather than by the slice—made it the perfect food for groups, whether coworkers, teammates, or families.

The American pizza landscape changed forever with the rise of chain restaurants. Pizza Hut was founded in Wichita, Kansas, in 1958, followed by Little Caesars in 1959, Domino's in 1960, and Papa John's in 1989. Unlike the traditional pizzerias that focused on craftsmanship, these chains prioritized efficiency and scalability. Their business models centered on mass production rather than preserving the authenticity of home-style pizza.

While chain pizzerias still made pizza by hand, they used pre-made dough, pre-packaged sauce, and centrally produced cheese, which diminished the artistry of the craft. Their lower prices and aggressive marketing made it difficult for independent pizzerias to compete. Between 1960 and 2000, the number of independently owned pizzerias declined dramatically, while the number of chain pizza outlets soared. For many Americans, their first experience with pizza came from a chain restaurant rather than a family-run pizzeria.

Luckily for me, I was not one of those people. My earliest memory of pizza dates back to my childhood, when my older sister Angela attended dance school on 13th Avenue in Brooklyn. Next door was a pizzeria named Krispy Pizza. During the warm weather months, when I tired of watching my sister and her classmates spin endlessly, I would stand at the counter and watch "Pete the Pizza Man" make pie after pie alongside his sons.

Krispy Pizza was a staple in my home. Every Friday was pizza night, and our regular order remains vivid in my memory: one Sicilian pie—half marinara with no cheese and mushrooms, the other half regular—and a spinach ring. My love for food was shaped by these moments, whether it was my parents' chocolate business, my grandmother's home cooking, or baking with my Aunt Ellen. Watching Pete and his sons work left an indelible impression on me, reinforcing my passion for food and, ultimately, my path to becoming a chef.

At the time, as a little boy barely able to see over the counter, I saw them simply as men making pizza. Now, as a culinary professional, I recognize that they were artists—engineers of flavor and texture. Most importantly, they were a father and sons, working together, bound by tradition and love for their craft. That devotion made their pizza taste even better. Decades later, Krispy Pizza is still going strong, not just on 13th Avenue but in several New Jersey locations as well.

There's nothing quite like Krispy's pizza, but for those who want to try making their own, here's my simplified recipe for delicious homemade pizza.

Homemade Pizza

Ingredients for Dough:

13 oz.	Water, lukewarm
0.1 oz.	Active dry yeast
20 oz.	Double Zero flour, plus extra for dusting
0.5 oz.	Sea salt

Ingredients for Pizza: *Yields 1 Pizza*

9 oz.	Pizza dough
As needed.	Flour, for dusting
3 oz.	Tomatoes, crushed
4 oz.	Fresh mozzarella, sliced thin
2 oz.	Extra Virgin Olive Oil
As needed.	Basil leaves, fresh for garnish

Instructions for Dough:

Add the water and yeast to a large bowl (or the bowl of a stand mixer) and whisk until thoroughly blended. Combine the flour and salt in a medium bowl, then add the flour mixture to the wet ingredients.

If using a mixer:

Fit the mixer with the dough hook and pour the flour and yeast mixture into the mixer bowl. Turn the machine on at a low speed for 5 to 10 minutes, or until it's firm and stretchy. Cover the dough with a dish towel and leave to rise in a warm place for about 2 hours, or until doubled in size.

If mixing by hand:

Stir with a wooden spoon until a dough starts to form. Continue mixing by hand until the pizza dough comes together in a ball. Place the dough onto a lightly-floured surface and knead with both hands for about 10 minutes, until it's firm and stretchy. Return the dough to the bowl. Cover with a dish towel and leave to rise in a warm place for about 2 hours, or until doubled in size.

Instructions for Pizza:

Preheat an oven or a pizza oven with a pizza stone to 500°F on the stone baking board inside. You can check the temperature inside your oven quickly and easily using an infrared thermometer.

Using a small amount of flour, dust your work surface and your pizza peel. Stretch the pizza dough ball out to 12 or 16 inches and lay it out on your pizza peel.

Top with sauce, followed by the mozzarella and olive oil, spreading both evenly on the dough and leaving room for the crust.

Slide the pizza off the peel and into your oven and cook for 1 to 2 minutes (depending on the oven), making sure to rotate the pizza every 20 seconds for an even bake.

Once cooked, remove the pizza from the oven and top with whole, fresh basil leaves.

Tip:

Make more dough than you need, or just want to have some on hand in a pinch? No problem. The best time to freeze your homemade pizza dough is after the first rise (after it's doubled in size). Once your dough has doubled in size, divide it into equal dough balls. Make sure you've put a light layer of olive oil into your containers to prevent the dough from sticking. Place the dough balls into separate containers with lids, and place in the freezer. You can freeze your dough balls for up to 3 months.

Mashed Potato

Ingredients: **Yields 10 Servings**

5 lbs.	Potatoes (half Russet and half Yukon Gold)
2	Garlic cloves, minced
To Taste.	Sea salt
6 Tbsp.	Unsalted butter
1 cup.	Whole milk
4 oz.	Whipped cream cheese, room temperature

Instructions:

Cut the potatoes. Feel free to peel your potatoes or leave the skins on. Then cut them into evenly-sized chunks, about an inch thick, and transfer them to a large stockpot full of cold water.

Once all of your potatoes are cut, be sure that there is enough cold water in the pan so that the water line sits about 1 inch above the potatoes. Stir the garlic and 1 tablespoon sea salt into the water. Then turn the heat to high and cook until the water comes to a boil. Reduce heat to medium-high (or whatever temperature is needed to maintain the boil) and continue cooking for about 10-12 minutes, or until a knife inserted in the middle of a potato goes in easily with almost no resistance. Carefully drain out all of the water.

Meanwhile, as the potatoes are boiling, heat the butter, milk and an additional 2 teaspoons of sea salt together either in a small saucepan or in the microwave until the butter is just melted. (You want to avoid boiling the milk.) Set aside until ready to use.

After draining the water, immediately return the potatoes to the hot stockpot, place it back on the hot burner, and turn the heat down to low. Using two oven mitts, carefully hold the handles on the stockpot and shake it gently on the burner for about 1 minute to help cook off some of the remaining steam within the potatoes. Remove the stockpot entirely from the heat and set it on a flat, heatproof surface.

Using your preferred kind of potato masher, mash the potatoes to your desired consistency.

Then pour half of the melted butter mixture over the potatoes, and fold it in with a wooden spoon or spatula until potatoes have soaked up the liquid. Repeat with the remaining butter, and then again with the cream cheese, folding in each addition in until just combined to avoid over-mixing. (Feel free to add in more warm milk to reach your desired consistency, if needed.)

One final time, taste the potatoes and season with extra salt if needed.

Chef Tips on Making the Perfect Mashed Potatoes...

1: Use a blend of potatoes. No matter who you ask each person will have a strong conviction on the type of potatoes to use when making mashed potatoes. Some variety gives the starchiness but not the creaminess and visa versa. It's best to use a 50/50 blend of Russet and Yukon gold to get the perfect consistency from both varieties.

2: Avoid water logging your potatoes. Many of us grew up watching our relatives boil who potatoes, but by boiling whole potatoes can often make them cook unevenly. Cut the potatoes into evenly sized smaller piece. Also to avoid water logging do not over boil your potatoes, as soon as a piece of potato can be easily pierced with a knife or fork they are done.

3: Dry the potatoes: Immediately after the potatoes have been drained return them to the same hot stockpot they were cooked in.Place the pot over a low heat on the stove. Hold the stock pot firmly and shake it for 2 to 3 minutes to release additional steam from the potatoes. Then remove the pan from the heat and set it aside, then your potatoes will be ready to be mashed.

4: Don't over mix! In general, you want to stir I the liquids into your masked potatoes until they are just combined. A mixture like made potatoes can only handle so much liquid once it reaches that capacity and additional liquids added the mashed potatoes will become gummy and have a terrible mouthfeel.

5: Season along the way! A general rule of thumb when cooking is to always taste and season along the way. As food cooked it is undergoing a change and with that change requires seasoning. To season mashed potatoes use sea salt and season both the water while they are boiling as well as afterwards when you are assembling them with butter, milk and cream cheese. Always season conservatively, seasoning can always be added, but can not be removed if overdone.

6: Equipment: Any recipe is easier when you have the right tools. Getting the type of masher that goes along with the type of mashed potatoes you like will make the task of making them easier, and quicker.

Baked Beans

Ingredients:

Yields 10 Servings

8 oz.	Bacon
45 oz.	Navy beans
15 oz.	Tomato sauce
¼ cup.	Tomato paste
¼ cup.	Apple cider vinegar
¼ cup.	Brown sugar
¼ cup.	Molasses
1 Tbsp.	Dijon mustard
2 tsp.	Worestchire sauce
2 tsp.	Smoked Paprika
1 tsp.	Garlic powder
½ tsp.	Onion powder
¼ tsp.	Cayenne pepper
¼ tsp.	Black pepper

Instructions:

Preheat the oven to 350°F. Cut the bacon into 1-inch pieces and cook in a skillet over medium heat until brown and crispy. Drain off all but 1-2 Tbsp of the bacon fat.

Drain the canned beans well, then add them to the skillet and stir to combine with the bacon.

Add the remaining ingredients: tomato sauce, tomato paste, apple cider vinegar, brown sugar, molasses, Dijon, Worcestershire sauce, smoked paprika, garlic powder, onion powder, cayenne and black pepper. Stir until everything is very well combined.

Bake the beans for 60-75 minutes, stirring once at 30 minutes and again at 60 minutes. If the sauce is thick at 60 minutes, it's done. If it's still a bit runny, bake 10-15 minutes longer.

Corn Dogs

German immigrants in the early 1920's brought sausages and Frankfurters with them to the United States, but weren't always well received by Americans. To make them more appealing some inventive cooks began coating sausage in different types of coatings and frying them. Ultimately, a corn battered Frankfurter or "hot dog" gained most popularity and the name corn dog was the label created for the new food item.In the 1940's brought the rise to state fairs across America. In 1942, the Texas State Fair is where the corn dog was introduced to the masses. The "Pronto Pup" and the "Fletcher's Corny Dogs' were among the first versions of the corn dog sold in mass at state fairs. "Pronto Pup" because of its quick way of cooking and the "Fletcher Corny Dogs" named after Carl and Neil Fletcher in Texas.

Ingredients:　　　　　　　　　　　　　　　　　　　　　　　　　　　　　　　　　　　　**Yields 10 servings**

3/4 cup.	Yellow cornmeal
3/4 cup.	Self-rising flour
1	Egg, large, room temperature, lightly beaten
2/3 cup.	Milk 2%
10	Wooden Sticks
10	Hot dogs
As needed.	Vegetable Oil, for frying

Instructions:

In a large bowl, combine cornmeal, flour and egg. Stir in milk to make a thick batter; let stand 4 minutes. Insert sticks into hot dogs; dip into batter.

In an electric skillet or deep-fat fryer, heat oil to 375°. Fry corn dogs, a few at a time, until golden brown, 6-8 minutes, turning occasionally. Drain on paper towels.

Southern Style Biscuits

Ingredients: **Yields 12 biscuits**

2 cups.	All-purpose flour
1/4 cup.	All purpose flour, for dusting
2 tsp.	Baking powder
1/2 tsp.	Baking soda
1/2 tsp.	Kosher salt
1 stick.	Unsalted butter, frozen and cut into cubes
1 cup.	Buttermilk

Instructions:

Arrange a rack in the middle of the oven and heat to 450°F.

Whisk 2 cups (10 ounces) all-purpose flour, 2 teaspoons baking powder, 1/2 teaspoon baking soda, and 1/2 teaspoon kosher salt together in a medium bowl; set aside.

Place a box grater over a small piece of parchment paper. Grate 1 stick (4 ounces) frozen unsalted butter on the large holes of a box grater. When you get down to a small nub of butter, chop that nub into 5 to 6 small pieces.

Use the piece of parchment paper to transfer the butter to the dry ingredients. Use your fingers to sift the butter into the flour and break up any clumps of grated butter.

Pour in 1 cup buttermilk and beat it in with a wooden spoon until the dough comes together and pulls away from the sides of the bowl.

Transfer the dough to a lightly floured cutting board. Pat the dough into a 1-inch-thick rough rectangle. Sprinkle the dough with a little more flour, if needed.

Fold the dough in half from top to bottom, then pat it back down into its original shape.

Repeat with the folding and patting, alternating folding from each side, the bottom, and the top until you have completed a total of 8 folds. At the end, the dough should be a little springy to the touch.

Pat the dough into a 1-inch thickness. Use a 3-inch round cutter to cut the dough into 6 biscuits. If you don't get 6 the first time around, refold and pat down the excess dough and cut more as needed. Discard the scraps of leftover dough.

Arrange the biscuits in a 10-inch cast iron skillet so that the biscuits touch each other, but not the sides of the pan. Put the skillet in the oven and increase the oven temperature to 500°F. Bake until the biscuits are golden-brown, 15 to 18 minutes.

Chicken Fried Steak with Gravy

Ingredients: **Yields 4 servings**

4	Beef cube steaks, 8 ounces each	4 cups.	Whole milk
2 ¼ cups.	All-purpose flour, divided	To taste.	Kosher Salt
2 tsp.	Baking powder		
1 tsp.	Baking soda		
1 tsp.	Black pepper		
¾ tsp.	Salt		
1 ½ cups.	Buttermilk		
1 Tbsp.	Tobasco sauce		
1	Egg, large		
2	Garlic cloves, minced		
3 cups.	Vegetable shortening for frying		

Instructions:

Place steaks between 2 layers of plastic and pound to a thickness of 1/4 inch.

Place 2 cups flour in a shallow bowl. Stir together baking powder, baking soda 1 teaspoon pepper, and ¾ teaspoon salt in second shallow bowl. Add buttermilk, Tabasco sauce, egg, and garlic; stir to combine. Heat shortening in a deep cast-iron skillet to 325 degrees F. Place a wire rack over a sheet of parchment paper.

While the shortening is heating, dredge a steak in flour to coat; shake off excess. Dip into buttermilk batter; lift up so excess batter drips back into the bowl. Press in flour again to coat both sides completely. Place breaded steak on the wire rack and repeat to bread remaining steaks.

Fry steaks, in batches if necessary, until evenly golden brown, 3 to 5 minutes per side. Remove steaks to a paper towel-lined plate to drain. Cover with foil to keep warm while you make the gravy.

Drain fat from the skillet, reserving ¼ cup of the liquid and as much of the solid remnants as possible.

Return the skillet to medium-low heat; add the reserved oil. Whisk the remaining ¼ cup flour into the oil. Scrape the bottom of the pan with a spatula to release solids into the gravy.

Stir in milk, increase the heat to medium, and bring the gravy to a simmer. Cook, stirring often, until thick, 6 to 7 minutes. Season with Kosher salt and pepper.

Steak au Poivre

Ingredients: **Yields 4 servings**

4	Tenderloin or Rib Eye steaks 1 ½ - 2 inches thick (8 oz each)
¼ cup.	Peppercorns, roughly crushed
1 Tbsp.	Olive oil
1 Tbsp.	Butter
¾ cup.	Cognac divided
1 ¼ cup.	Heavy cream
1	Garlic clove, minced
1 tsp.	Thyme
½ tsp.	Beef base
To Taste.	Salt

Instructions:

Pull the steaks out of the refrigerator at least 30 minutes before cooking. Sprinkle generously with salt on all sides.

Set the pepper grinder on the largest setting. Grind the pepper into very coarse pieces. If you find your pepper grinder settings are small, you can pour the peppercorns into a mortar and pestle and crush them into large coarse pieces.

Pour the cracked peppercorns on a plate. Press the steaks into the peppercorns on both sides. Shake the plate in between to make sure they coat evenly.

Set a large cast-iron skillet over medium heat. Once hot, place the olive oil and butter into the skillet. Once the butter melts, add the steaks to the skillet and sear for 4 to 5 minutes per side. (Four minutes for 1 ½-inch steaks, five minutes for 2-inch steaks.)

Move the steaks to a holding plate and cover with foil. Carefully pour ½ cup cognac into the hot skillet. Slightly tip the pan so the Cognac catches the flame. Allow the alcohol to burn off, shaking the pan as needed until the flame dies.

Pour the heavy cream into the skillet, followed by the minced garlic, dried thyme, and beef base. Whisk well and allow the cream to come to a gentle simmer. Simmer for 4 to 5 minutes until the sauce slightly thickens.

Taste, then add 1 to 4 more tablespoons of Cognac, to taste. Salt as needed.

Serve the steaks warm with a hearty spoonful of peppery Cognac sauce over the top.

Chicken Parmesan

Ingredients: **Yields 2 Servings**

2	Chicken breasts, boneless, skinless and thinly pounded
½ cup.	Italian seasoned breadcrumbs
¼ cup.	Panko breadcrumbs
¼ cup.	Parmesan cheese, freshly grated
¼ tsp.	Garlic powder
¼ tsp.	Black pepper, freshly ground
2	Egg whites
4 oz.	Mozzarella, fresh
½ cup.	Tomato Sauce
For garnish.	Fresh basil, sliced thin

Instructions:

Preheat your oven to 400°F. Lightly coat a baking sheet with cooking spray. Cut each chicken breast in half lengthwise, so you have 4 pieces total. Pound each piece to an even 1/2-inch thickness. Set aside.

In a wide, shallow bowl (a pie dish works well), combine the Italian breadcrumbs, whole wheat Panko breadcrumbs, Parmesan, garlic powder, and pepper. In a separate bowl, whisk together the egg whites until lightly foamy. Cut the mozzarella into 4 slices, or grate and divide into four equal portions.

Arrange your workstation in the following order: pounded chicken, egg whites, breadcrumb mixture, then the baking sheet. Working one at a time, dip each piece of chicken into the egg whites, shaking off any excess, then the breadcrumbs, gently patting the chicken as needed so that the crumbs stick to all sides.

Place on the prepared baking sheet. Lightly coat the tops of the chicken with cooking spray. Bake until the chicken reaches an internal temperature of 160°F (use an instant-read thermometer to check for doneness) and the crumbs are brown, about 15 minutes.

Remove from the oven, spoon 2 tablespoons of sauce over each piece of chicken, and top with a slice of mozzarella cheese. Return to the oven and bake until the cheese is melted, about 3-5 additional minutes.

Sprinkle with basil and enjoy immediately, topped with extra sauce as desired.

Baked Ziti

Ingredients: **Yields 4 servings**

1 lb.	Ziti pasta noodles
1½ lbs.	Italian sausage
4	Garlic cloves, minced
28 oz.	Tomatoes, crushed
1 tsp.	Salt
1½ tsp.	Sugar (optional)
¼ tsp.	Red pepper flakes, crushed
1 cup.	Heavy cream
⅓ cup.	Pecorino Romano cheese
⅓ cup.	Basil, chopped
2 cups.	Mozzarella, shredded

Instructions:

Bring a large pot of salted water to a boil. Add the 1 lb of ziti noodles and cook according to the package directions for very al dente, about 7 minutes. (It will continue to cook in the oven so you want to undercook it just a bit.) Drain and add the pasta back to the pot. Set aside.

Preheat the oven to 425°F and set the oven rack in the middle position.

Heat a large sauté pan (preferably nonstick) over medium-high heat. Crumble the 1½ lbs of sausage into the pan and cook, breaking apart with a wooden spoon, until lightly browned and just cooked through, 5 to 6 minutes. Use a slotted spoon to transfer the cooked sausage to a plate. Drain all but 1 tablespoon of the fat from the pan and set over low heat (if you don't have enough fat in the pan, add a tablespoon of olive oil). Add the 4 cloves of minced garlic and cook, stirring constantly with a wooden spoon, until soft but not browned, about 1 minute. Add the 28-oz can of crushed tomatoes, 1 teaspoon salt, 1½ teaspoons sugar and ¼ teaspoon red pepper flakes and simmer, uncovered, for 10 minutes.

Add the 1 cup cream, ⅓ cup of the Pecorino Romano, cooked sausage, and ⅓ cup basil to the pan; stir until evenly combined. Carefully pour the contents of the sauté pan into the large pot with the pasta and gently stir to combine. Spoon half of the mixture into a 9 x 13-inch baking dish. Sprinkle with half of the shredded mozzarella (1 cup) and half the remaining Pecorino Romano (1½ tablespoons). Spoon the remaining pasta mixture on top and sprinkle with the remaining mozzarella (1 cup) and Pecorino Romano (1½ tablespoons). Transfer to the oven and bake, uncovered, until the cheese has melted and browned, 15 to 20 minutes. Sprinkle with more basil and serve.

Classic Grilled Cheese

Yield: 1 sandwich

Ingredients:

1/2 Tbsp.	Unsalted butter
2 oz.	Cheddar or sliced American cheese
2 slices.	Sandwich bread, sliced
1 tsp.	Mayonnaise

Instructions:

Place 1/2 tablespoon unsalted or salted butter on the counter and let sit at room temperature until softened. Alternatively, place in a microwave-safe bowl and microwave just until slightly softened and spreadable, 5 to 10 seconds. Meanwhile, grate 2 ounces sharp cheddar cheese on the large holes of a box grater if needed (about 1/2 cup).

Spread the butter onto one side of each of 2 slices white sandwich bread. Spread 1 teaspoon mayonnaise in an even layer over the buttered bread. Flip 1 slice of the bread over and top with the cheddar or 2 ounces sliced American cheese (2 to 3 slices) in an even layer. Top with the second slice of bread, buttered-side up.

Heat a small skillet over medium-low heat. Place the sandwich in the skillet. Cover and cook until the bottom is golden-brown and the cheese is partially melted, 2 to 4 minutes. Flip and cook uncovered until the second side is golden-brown and the cheese is completely melted, 1 to 2 minutes more.

New England Clam Chowder

Ingredients for the Chowder: **Yields: 2 servings**

13 oz.	Clam meat, chopped	¼ tsp.	Kosher salt
16 oz.	Clam juice	To taste.	Black pepper, freshly ground
1	White onion, chopped fine	To taste.	Salt
2	Yukon Gold potatoes, peeled and diced		
1 cup.	Half and Half		
2	Bacon slices, chopped fine		
2 Tbsp.	Unsalted butter		
1 Tbsp.	All Purpose flour		

For garnish:

Chopped chives
Chowder crackers

Instructions :

Drain the canned clams and set aside, saving the juice.

Add the liquid drained from the clams and the bottled clam juice to a medium saucepan.

Heat to a boil and add the chopped onion and diced potatoes.

Cook over medium heat until the potatoes are fork tender and the liquid has reduced. Skim off and discard any foam that develops on top.

Cook the diced bacon in a small skillet until crispy. Remove the bacon and keep the bacon grease.

Add the butter to the bacon grease and heat until the butter melts.

Add the flour a little bit at a time whisking constantly. Cook for one minute but do not allow the roux to brown. You want a light roux for this soup.

Add the half and half to the soup pot and heat to a simmer. Add the roux to the soup and cook until thick.

Add the chopped clams and bacon. Cook until the clams are heated through.

Add salt and pepper to taste. Serve hot with chopped chives and chowder crackers on top.

Chicken Wings

Yields 2 servings

Ingredients:

3 Tbsp.	Olive oil
3	Garlic cloves, pressed
2 tsp.	Chili powder
1 tsp.	Garlic powder
To taste.	Salt
To taste.	Black pepper
10	Chicken wings

Instructions:

Preheat the oven to 375 degrees F.

Combine olive oil, garlic, chili powder, garlic powder, salt, and pepper in a large, resealable bag; seal and shake to combine. Add chicken wings; reseal and shake to coat. Arrange chicken wings on a baking sheet.

Cook chicken wings in the preheated oven until crisp and cooked through, about 30 to 45 minutes.

Did You Know...?

The chicken wing was created in 1964 by Teressa Bellissomo in Buffalo, New York. Before Bellissomo fried some chicken wings as a late night snack, chicken wings were only used as chicken parts used for making stocks and soups. The original wings she created was dressed with a combination of hot sauce and melted butter. For a long time they were only named Buffalo wings because of where they were created. When they gained popularity in the 1970's many other cultures used chicken wings to make their own adaptation of the dish often changing the sauce to make it more culturally associated. Jerk chicken wings are associated with Jamaica, Yangnyeom are associated with Korea, the flavor of Lemon pepper associated with United States City Atlanta, Garlic Parmesan is associated with Italy. In 1982 with the opening of Buffalo Wild Wings and in 1983 with the opening of Hooters chicken wings became a top menu item for both and became a fan favorite associated with large sports events like the Super Bowl when Americans consume an estimated 1.4 billion chicken wings just on that day alone.

Oven Baked Nachos

Ingredients:

1 lb.	Beef, ground
2 Tbsp.	Taco seasoning
1 bag.	Tortilla chips
15 oz.	Black beans, drained
8 oz.	Cheddar cheese, shredded
8 oz.	Mexican cheese blend, shredded
15 oz.	Refried beans

Optional Toppings:

11 oz.	Corn
1 cup.	Tomatoes, chopped into cubes
3 Tbsp.	Red onions finely diced
2	Jalapenos seeded and diced or sliced
As needed.	Sour cream
4 Tbsp.	Cilantro, chopped fine
2.	Green onions, sliced
1	Avocado sliced or diced
15 oz.	Black olives, sliced
13 oz.	Salsa
As needed.	Lime wedges

Yields 8 servings

Instructions:

Cook ground beef in skillet on stovetop until no pink remains.

Sprinkle with taco seasoning and continue cooking for 1-2 minutes. Add 1-2 tablespoons of water if necessary. Drain and set aside.

Preheat oven to 375 degrees F and spray a baking cookie sheet with non-stick cooking spray.

Add tortilla chips to prepared baking sheet.

Spoon refried beans over chips.

Add half of the ground beef mixture over refried beans.

Add half of the cheddar and Mexican blend cheeses.

Spoon remaining ground beef mixture over cheese.

Top with black beans. Sprinkle remaining cheeses over beans

Bake in oven for 10-15 minutes or until cheese is melted and bubbly. Add whatever optional toppings you would like at this time.

Fish and Chips
A Tasty History

The pairing of fish and chips has long been considered a British staple. The irresistible combination of a hunk of battered cod resting atop a mound of steaming hot chips (french fries in America) is the quintessential British comfort food. Whether eaten on a plastic tray on your lap in front of the "telly" or gobbled down from a makeshift paper cone on the way home from the pub, a meal of fish and chips is like a serving of deep fried nostalgia in the UK – and let's not forget a sprinkling of salt and vinegar.

At the dish's peak of popularity in the late 1920s, there were 35,000 fish and chips shops in the United Kingdom (England, Scotland, Wales, and Northern Ireland). Today, there are still 10,500 "chippies" in the U.K. serving 360 million meals of fish and chips every year. That's the equivalent of six servings of fish and chips to every British man, woman, and child.

The golden fried combo is so deeply entrenched in British culture that it can be hard to imagine a time when there wasn't a fish and chip shop in every neighborhood. But travel back a mere 200 years and you would be hard pressed to find a combination of fried fish and chipped potatoes anywhere in the British Isles. Yes, the origin story of fish and chips is a bit more complex than the nationalist sentiment might imply.

Food history tells us that it all began outside the U.K hundreds of years ago. From the 8th to the 12th centuries, Jews, Muslims, and Christians lived in relative peace in Portugal, known as Al-Andalus, under Moorish rule. Sephardic Jews, who likely comprised 20 percent of the population, held positions in the high court. But the strength of Moorish rule diminished over time as Christian armies started conquering the territory. By 1249, Moorish rule ended in Portugal

The situation changed dramatically in the 15th century. First, the Spanish Inquisition outlawed Judaism, sending Spanish Jews fleeing to neighboring Portugal. Then in 1496, the Portuguese King Manuel I married Isabella of Spain who was not on board with religious freedom. She insisted on the expulsion of all Jews from Portugal. Manuel I mandated that all Jews be baptized or otherwise be expelled.

While many fled, some Jews stayed and either converted to Christianity or pretended to do so while continuing to practice Judaism in secret. But when Portugal fell under Spanish rule, the Inquisition targeted individuals with Jewish lineage threatening anyone claiming to be a "converso." As religious violence worsened, many chose to flee to other parts of Europe with large numbers settling in England. As with many cultures, wherever the Sephardic Jews traveled they brought their rich culinary traditions.

Cooking is not allowed on the Jewish Sabbath (Shabbat) which begins on sundown Friday night and ends on sundown Saturday. So Sephardic Jewish families would prepare food on Friday afternoon that would last the next 24 hours. One of those dishes was a white fish, typically cod or haddock, fried in a thin coat of flour or matzo meal. The batter preserved the fish so it could be eaten cold and without sacrificing too much flavor for the next day.

It was a hit. Soon, Jewish immigrants to England took to selling fried fish in the streets from trays hung from their necks by leather straps. As early as 1781, a British cookbook refers to "the Jews' way of preserving all sorts of fish," and Thomas Jefferson, after a visit to England, wrote about sampling "fried fish in the Jewish fashion."

In his London based novel Oliver Twist (1837), Charles Dickens refers to "fried fish warehouses," the forerunner to the modern chippie where bread or baked potato were served alongside the fish.

A little later, in 1845, cook and writer Alenis Soyer in his first edition of A Shilling Cooking for the People gave a recipe for "Fried Fish, Jewish Fashion" which was fish dipped into a batter of flour and water and then fried.

But it wasn't until the latter part of the 19th century that Jewish fried fish fully made the cultural transfer from the streets of London to the broader British populace. And for that food historians credit two developments. First, the advent of industrial scale trawl fishing in the North Sea meant that inexpensive fish could be transported to all corners of the U.K. by the second development, extensive railroad lines. Fried fish consumption rocketed with these technological advances.

That basically covers the fish bit, but what about the second half of the dish?

Nobody is entirely sure how fried potatoes became a part of the European diet. Food historians do know that it took a really long time for fried potatoes (or potatoes of any kind) to make their way to England.

Belgium stakes a claim as the inventor of fried potatoes. The story goes that in 1680 winter was so cold that the River Meuse (located in present day Belgium) froze over and that the women in the area would turn to cutting potatoes in the shape of fish and frying them in a bit of oil so as to provide sustenance for their families.

Going back to Charles Dickens, he mentions in his 1859 novel A Tale of Two Cities, "husky chips of potato fried with some reluctant drops of oil," which means that chips had definitely reached England by mid-century.

It is difficult to pinpoint the precise arrival of fried potatoes in England, but by 1860 we see the very first fish and chips shops.

As usual with food origins, there are competing claims for being the first British fish and chip shop.

Many food historians say that a Jewish cook, a young Ashkenezi immigrant named Joseph Malin, opened the first chippy in 1860 in London. The shop was so successful that it remained in business until the 1970s. And up near Manchester, the fish and chip stand opened by John Lees was doing a brisk business by 1863.

By 1910 there were 25,000 fish and chip shops in the U.K. and they even stayed open during World War I. In an effort to boost morale at home, Prime Minister David Lloyd George made sure that fish and chips stayed off the ration list (eggs, bread, and meat were on the list). The same practice was observed during World War II, when Winston Churchill famously referred to a hot meal of fish and chips as "the good companions."

Fish and Chips

Yields 6 servings

Ingredients for Fish:

2 ¼ lbs.	Cod fish filet
1 cup.	All purpose flour, for dusting
As needed.	Vegetable oil, for frying

Ingredients for Batter:

1 Cup.	All Purpose Flour
¼ cup.	Cornmeal
1½ tsp.	Baking Powder
1 tsp.	Salt
½ tsp.	Black pepper
½ tsp.	Paprika
1 cup.	Seltzer water, ice cold

Ingredients for Chips:

2 ¼ lb.	Russet Potatoes
As needed.	Vegetable oil

Instructions for Chips:

Cut potatoes into fries and blanch them in hot water for 7-10 minutes. Drain them in colander.

In a deep pot or fryer heat the oil to 350 degrees F. Deep fry them in hot oil until golden brown. Put them in a tray and put them in the oven to keep crispy and hot.

Instructions for Fish:

Pat the fish dry. Cut and trim it into desired size ensuring they all roughly the same size.

In a mixing bowl whisk together the flour, cornmeal, baking powder salt, pepper and paprika. Add cold soda water into the batter and whisk just until incorporated into the flour. Do not over-mix, it's ok to have lumps in the flour. The batter should be thin, dripping consistency. If too thick, add little more
soda water.

Heat oil on medium heat. To test the oil temperature put a drop of batter in the oil. If it floats and puffs up immediately it means oil is hot enough.

Dredge the fish in dry flour and shake off the excess. Dip it into the batter and carefully lower it in hot oil. Don't over crowd the pot, cook in batches. Cook until golden brown. Drain on the paper towel or wire rack.

Serve immediately with chips, lemon wedges and tartare sauce on the side.

Chicken Nuggets

Ingredients: **Yields 6 servings**

3	Chicken breasts, boneless and skinless
1 cup.	Italian seasoned bread crumbs
½ cup.	Parmesan cheese, grated
1 Tbsp.	Dried Basil
1 tsp.	Dried Thyme
1 tsp.	Salt
½ cup.	Unsalted butter, melted

Instructions:

Preheat the oven to 400 degrees F.

Cut chicken breasts into 1 ½-inch pieces. Mix the bread crumbs, Parmesan, basil, thyme, and salt together well in a medium bowl. Put melted butter in a bowl or dish for dipping.

Dip chicken pieces into the melted butter first, then coat with the bread crumb mixture. Place the well-coated chicken nuggets on a lightly greased cookie sheet in a single layer.

Bake nuggets in the preheated oven until browned and chicken is cooked through, about 20 minutes.

Fun Facts About The Chicken Nugget...

1: The chicken nugget was invented in the 1950's by a food science professor at Cornell University named Robert C. Baker

2: Baker originally named the chicken nugget "chicken crispies" to make them more appealing and to boost poultry consumption in the United States.

3: Baker never patented his idea, he shared it freely for public benefit.

4: In 1983, McDonald's introduced the Chicken McNugget under culinary direction of Chef René Arend.

5: When McDonald's launched the McNugget, it became so famous so quickly, McDonald's had to ration them to select locations due to supply shortages.

6: The World Record for eating the most chicken nuggets in three minutes was set by Leah Shutkever in 2020 consulting 1.7 pounds of nuggets.

Cheese Perogies with Bacon and Onions

Yields 4 servings

Ingredients for Dough:

2 cups.	All-purpose flour
1 tsp.	Kosher salt
2 Tbsp.	Salted butter, melted
1 cup.	Greek yogurt, full fat
1	Egg, large

Ingredients for the Filling:

4	Russet potatoes, peeled and quartered
2 Tbsp.	Salted butter, at room temperature
2 cups.	Cheddar cheese, shredded
2 oz.	Cream cheese
To taste.	Kosher salt
To taste.	Black pepper

Ingredients for Onion Butter Sauce:

4 slices.	bacon, thick cut and chopped
4 Tbsp.	Salted butter
2	Yellow onions, thinly sliced
3 Tbsp.	Apple cider vinegar
1 Tbsp.	1Thyme leaves, fresh

Instructions:

To make the dough. In a medium bowl, combine the flour, salt, butter, yogurt, and egg, and mix until combined. Knead the dough for 2-3 minutes. Cover and let sit 30 minutes.

To make the filling. Bring the potatoes to a boil in a large pot of cold water. Salt the water and cook until the potatoes are tender, about 20 to 30 minutes.

Drain the potatoes, return the potatoes to the pot and mash over low heat, adding the butter, cheddar cheese, and cream cheese. Season to taste with salt and pepper.

Roll the dough out onto a floured surface to 1/8 inch thickness. Using a biscuit cutter, cut out 3-inch circles. Spoon 2 teaspoons of filling into the center of each round. Brush the edges with water and fold half of the dough over the filling to enclose it. Press down the edges to seal, pressing out all the air. Be sure to keep the dough covered as you work to prevent from drying out. At this point, the pierogi can be flash-frozen on a baking sheet for 30 minutes, then transferred to a freezer bag and frozen for up to 3 months.

When ready to cook, bring a large pot of salted water to a boil. Boil the pierogies in batches for 2-3 minutes, or until they float. Drain. To make the butter sauce, cook the bacon in a large skillet over medium heat until crisp. Drain onto a paper towel. Wipe the skillet clean, then set back over medium-high heat and melt 1 tablespoon butter.

Add the onions and cook 5 minutes, until softened. Add the apple cider, season with salt and pepper and continue cooking another 5-8 minutes, until the cider has evaporated and the onions are golden and caramelized. Add the remaining butter and thyme and cook 2-3 minutes, until the butter is browned. Remove from the heat.

Drop the pierogies into the sauce, gently tossing to combine. Spoon the pierogies and onions onto plates. Top with cheddar and bacon.

Chili

Ingredients:

Yields 6 servings

1 Tbsp.	Olive oil
1	White onion diced
2	Jalapeno peppers diced fine
6	Garlic
2 oz	Beef, ground
3 Tbsp.	Chili powder
1 Tbsp.	Cumin, ground
1 tsp.	Cayenne pepper
To taste.	Salt
To Taste.	Black pepper
2 Tbsp.	Tomato paste
1 ½ cups.	Beef broth
15 oz.	Tomatoes with juices, diced
15 oz.	Tomatoes with juices, crushed
30 oz.	Kidney beans drained and rinsed

Instructions:

Heat the oil in a large pot over medium heat. Add the onion and peppers and cook 2-3 minutes to soften. Add the garlic and cook for 1 minute. Add the ground beef and break apart with a wooden spoon. Brown the meat for 5-6 minutes, stirring occasionally.

Stir in the chili powder, ground cumin, cayenne, salt and pepper to taste, and tomato paste. Cook 1-2 minutes to let the spices bloom.

Add the beef broth, tomatoes, and kidney beans.

Bring to a boil, then reduce heat and simmer, uncovered, for at least 30 minutes to let the flavors mingle and develop.

You can simmer longer if you'd like, up to 60 minutes.

Serve with your favorite chili toppings, like shredded cheddar cheese, spicy chili flakes, sour cream, chopped green onion, chopped cilantro or parsley, or tortilla chips.

Drunken Meatloaf

Yields 6 servings

Ingredients:

1 Tbsp.	Olive oil
3 cups.	Yellow onions, chopped fine
1 tsp.	Thyme leaves, chopped fresh
2 tsp.	Kosher salt
1 tsp.	Black pepper
3 Tbsp.	Worcestershire sauce
1/3 cup.	Chicken stock or broth
1 Tbsp.	Tomato paste
2 1/2 lbs.	Beef chuck
1/2 cup.	Bread crumbs
2	Eggs, beaten
1/2 cup.	Ketchup
1 cup.	Maker's Mark

Instructions:

Preheat the oven to 325 degrees F.

Heat the olive oil in a medium sauté pan. Add the onions, thyme, salt, and pepper and cook over medium-low heat, stirring occasionally, for 8 to 10 minutes, until the onions are translucent but not brown. Off the heat, add the Worcestershire sauce, chicken stock, and tomato paste. Allow to cool slightly.

In a large bowl, combine the ground chuck, onion mixture, bread crumbs, and eggs, and mix lightly with a fork. Don't mash or the meat loaf will be dense. Shape the mixture into a rectangular loaf on a sheet pan covered with parchment paper. Spread the ketchup evenly on top. Bake for 1 to 1 1/4 hours, until the internal temperature is 160 degrees F and the meat loaf is cooked through.

Chef Tip:

A pan of hot water in the oven, under the meat loaf, will keep the top from cracking.

Roasted Chicken

Ingredients: Yields 4 - 6 servings

1	Roasting chicken, whole, about 3 ½ pounds
3 Tbsp.	Unsalted butter, melted
1 tsp.	Salt
½ tsp.	Black pepper
1 bunch	Fresh thyme
1	Garlic head, sliced in half horizontally
½	White onion

Instructions:

Preheat the oven to 400°F.

Pat the chicken dry with paper towel, remove the giblets, tuck the chicken wings underneath the breast and tie the legs together with kitchen twine.

In a small bowl, combine the melted butter, salt, pepper and thyme. Use your hands to rub the butter mixture all over the chicken, making sure to get underneath the skin as well.

Stuff the garlic, onion and thyme sprigs inside the chicken cavity.

Place the chicken on a large baking dish and roast in the oven breast side up until the skin is golden brown and a thermometer inserted in the chicken reads 165°F, about 60-75 minutes. Spoon the juices from the bottom of the baking dish over the chicken and allow the chicken to rest for 15 minutes before carving.

Chef Tips To Roasting A Chicken

Tip No. 1 Tempering food is a simple but critical step that involves bringing an ingredient to room temperature prior to cooking so that it cooks more evenly. Tempering is important with most proteins, but it is essential when oven roasting large cuts of meat because it allows the protein to cook more effenticly.

Tip No. 2 Don't just throw your chicken into the oven - take a moment to truss the chicken. Tieing the legs up to help the thighs brown and removing the wing tips which have a tendcey to burn. If you prefer to leave the wingtips on cover them with foil or parchment paper, you can also tuck the wing tips underneath the shoulders to prevent them from burning. Some people like to spatchcock their chicken, or butterfly it so the bird can lay flat on the baking sheet. This increases the chickens surface area for a faster and more even cooking.

Tip No. 3 One way to deal with the fact that different parts of the chicken cook differently, is to take advantage of the fact that different parts of the oven are hot than others; the back of the oven tends to be hotter then the front. Position your chicken in the very back corner of your oven with the legs pointing straight into the corner and the breast pointing toward the center of the oven. Halfway through the cooking process, switch the chicken to the other corner so that the left and right sides of the bird are cooked evenly. Keep the breast of the chicken always pointing towards the center of the oven.

Tip No. 5: High oven temperatures will cause the chicken to brown but can also lead to overcooking. To prevent this apart your chicken in a hot oven. Once the chicken starts to brown lower the temperature to allow the bird to cook throughout and the chicken will remain at the perfect temperature.

Tip No. 6 Always make the chicken rest before carving into it. For the average three to four pound chicken resting at least ten minutes is ideal.

How Long Should You Roast Your Chicken?

The cooking time will depend on your oven temperature and the size of the chicken. The best way to gauge the actual temperature of the oven is it use an oven thermometer. Roasting a chicken is generally best between 350 degrees to 450 degrees F. If you are using a convection oven which uses fans to circulate the hot air consider reducing your temperature by 25 degrees and check your chicken more frequently.

As for the size of your chicken, larger cuts of meat take longer to cook and bone in cuts like a whole chicken need additional time because the bones and the sheer size create insulation which slows the cooking process down. Even if your oven is on a high temperature a larger bird will always take longer to roast than a small one.

How To Test If A Chicken Is Cooked:

There are three easy ways to tell if a chicken is cooked:

I. If you have a thermometer, a digital one preferably you can place the thermometer in the center of the breast and the thigh. If it reads 160 degrees F the chicken is fully cooked.

II. To check if your chicken is ready without the se of a thermometer give one of the legs a wiggle. It should've around freely and feel like it would easily separate from the rest of the chicken. This is also an excellent indication the chicken is fully cooked.

III. Stick a knife into the thigh area of the chicken, if the juices of the chicken are clear your chicken is fully cooked.

Roasted Chicken A Universally Embraced Dish

Roasted chicken is a universally cherished dish, found in almost every culture with countless variations in flavor, technique and presentation. Its global appeal stems from its simplicity and adaptability, allowing each region to infuse local ingredients and traditions into the preparations. While the core concept remains the same - cooking a whole chicken with dry heat - the diversity in marinades, spices, rubs and cooking methods makes each version distinct and reflective of its cultural roots.

The technique of roasting proteins is one of the earliest cooking methods known to humankind. Chicken was domesticated in Southeast Asia and India and became a favored protein because of its size and manageability.

Poulet Rôti is the classic French roasted chicken seasoned with herbs de Provence, garlic, butter and lemon. Typically roasted whole and served with its pan juices, roasted potatoes and a seasonal vegetable.

Pollo a la Brasa is the beloved Peruvian version of marinated with garlic, cumin, soy sauce, paprika and vinegar and then roasted over charcoal. Characterized by a smoky flavor and served with French fries, salad and a spicy traditional sauce called ají.

Tandoori Chicken from India is marinated in yogurt, ginger, garlic and a blend of spices typically tumeric, chili and garam masala. Traditionally roasted in a tandoor, a traditional clay oven for a charred and smoky taste. This roasted chicken often looks bright red in color due to the spiced placed in the yogurt marinade. The yogurt is used because it has enzymes that allow the chicken to break down and become more tender as it sits in the marinade.

Pakistan offers their version of roasted chicken with Zafrani Murgh, a royal style roasted chicken infused with saffrom, yogurt, cardamom and ghee and slowly roasted to absorb as much of the flavoring agents as possible and is typically served with naan or Pulao rice.

Asian countries like Thailand offers Kai Yang a roasted chicken marinated in fish sauce, garlic, cilantro root and white pepper and usually served with a sweet chili dipping sauce while the Philippines gives us Lechon Manok marinated in calamansi juice, soy sauce, garlic, lemongrass and annatto oil an roasted on a spit.

No matter where you are in the world a wide variety of cultural denominations have recognized roasted chicken as a guilty pleasure and comforting food while simultaneously allowing their own cultures to shine through to add to this universally loved dish.

Chapter Two
Sweet

Classic Vanilla Cupcakes

Ingredients Vanilla Cupcakes: **Yields 12 cupcakes**

1 ⅔ cup.	All-purpose flour
1 ½ tsp.	Baking powder
½ tsp.	Salt
1 cup.	Granulated sugar
½ cup.	Unsalted butter melted and slightly cooled
1	Egg, large
¼ cup.	Sour cream
¾ cup.	Whole Milk
2 tsp.	Pure vanilla extract

Ingredients for Vanilla Buttercream Frosting:

¾ cup.	Unsalted butter room temperature
3-4 cups.	Confectioners sugar
2 tsp.	Pure vanilla extract
3 Tbsp.	Whole Milk
⅛ tsp.	Kosher salt

Instructions Vanilla Cupcakes:

In a medium-sized bowl, whisk together flour, baking powder and salt.

In a large mixing bowl whisk the sugar and melted butter until smooth (mixture will be gritty). Whisk in eggs, then sour cream, milk and vanilla extract until combined.

Slowly add in dry ingredients and stir until completely incorporated. Batter will be thick.

Fill cupcake lines ⅔ of the way full (about ¼ cup of batter). Bake in the preheated oven for about 20 minutes or until a toothpick inserted in the center comes out clean.

Cool completely before frosting.

Instructions for Vanilla Buttercream Frosting:

Using a stand mixer with the whisk attachment (or a large mixing bowl and a handheld mixer), beat butter at medium speed until smooth and creamy; 2-3 minutes.

Add confectioners sugar, vanilla and milk. Turn mixer up to high speed and beat for 3 minutes. If mixture is too thick, add more milk, a teaspoon at a time. If too thin, add more confectioners sugar, a little at a time.

Frost cooled cupcakes using a spreader or a piping bag. Depending on how much frosting you use on each cupcake, there may be some leftover.

New York Style Cheesecake

Ingredients for Crust:

2 cups.	Graham cracker crumbs
1/3 cup.	Granulated sugar
1/2 cup.	Unsalted butter, melted
1/2 tsp.	Cinnamon, ground
1/8 tsp.	Salt

Ingredients for Cheesecake:

32 oz.	Cream cheese, at room temperature
1 1/2 cups.	Granulated sugar
3 Tbsp.	Cornstarch
4	Eggs, large room temperature
1	Egg yolk, room temperature
2 tsp.	Lemon juice
2 tsp.	Vanilla extract
1 cup	Sour cream

Yields 1 - 9 inch Cheesecake

Ingredients for Raspberry Sauce (Optional):

6 oz.	Raspberries (or frozen and thawed)
1/3 cup.	Granulated sugar
3 Tbsp.	Water
1 tsp.	Lemon juice

Instructions for Raspberry Sauce:

Add all ingredients to a saucepan over medium heat. Allow it to bubble and begin to mash the raspberries as they soften. Cook for about 20 minutes or until the mixture coats the back of a spoon. Pour it in to a heat safe container and chill before serving.

Instructions for Graham Cracker Crust:

Preheat your oven to 350F and prepare your 9 inch springform pan. Lightly coat the entire inside with cooking spray and place two strips (or as many as it takes to cover the walls) of parchment paper up against the sides. They should peak over top the pan just a little.

In a small bowl, mix together the graham cracker crumbs (finely ground in a food processor), sugar, melted butter, cinnamon, and salt. Combine until you get the texture of wet sand then poor it into the pan. Firmly press it down into the bottom and up the sides of the pan. It should almost reach the top.

Bake for 10 minutes then set it out to cool while you prepare the cheesecake.

Instructions for Cheesecake:

Drop the oven temperature to 305F and place a large baking pan on the very bottom rack of your oven. I just used a 9×13 baking pan. While you prepare the cheesecake, get a medium sized pot of water boiling over the stove. You'll pour this into the baking pan once you're ready to bake.

Before you start, make sure your cream cheese and eggs are at room temperature.

For best results, I highly recommend using a stand mixer. A hand mixer is also an option, but be very careful and only work on low speed.

In a small bowl, mix together the eggs, lemon juice, and vanilla with a fork. Set aside.

With the paddle attachment, mix the room temperature cream cheese on medium-low speed just until it's smooth (30 seconds to 1 minute). Add in the sugar and cornstarch and mix on low for about 30 seconds.

Stop and let it sit for a couple minutes, scrape down the sides and bottom of the bowl, then mix again for another 30 seconds or until it comes together.

With the mixer on the lowest setting, slowly add in the egg mixture in three to four additions slowly. Keep the mixer on low while mixing.

Take the bowl off the mixer and use a rubber spatula to fold in the sour cream. Pour the batter into the pan once the crust is cooled and tap the pan against your counter a couple times to bring up any air bubbles that might have been caught in the batter. Place the cheesecake on the middle rack and carefully pour the boiling water into the pan below. (If you don't have two racks, place the rack in the middle of the oven and wrap the base of the cheesecake pan in foil. Place it into the roast pan before pouring in the water).

Bake for an hour and 40 minutes. It will puff up a little in the oven but will come back down when it's cooling. Once it's done, leave the cheesecake in the oven, turn off the oven, and crack the door open. Let it sit in there for an hour.

After the hour is up, put the cheesecake in the refrigerator uncovered and let it chill overnight. The next day, remove the springform pan, slice, and top with your homemade raspberry sauce, powdered sugar, or leave it as is.

Brownies

Ingredients:

Yields 16 Brownies

12 Tbsp.	Unsalted butter, cubed
8 oz.	Dark chocolate, chopped
1 cup.	Granulated sugar
½ cup.	Light brown sugar, packed
3	Eggs, large
⅓ cup.	Cocoa powder
1 cup.	All-purpose flour
¾ tsp.	Salt
1 cup.	Dark chocolate, chips or chunks

Instructions:

Preheat the oven to 350 degrees and line an 8 x 8 pan with parchment paper leaving an overhang on 2 sides or spray the pan with cooking spray.

Combine butter and chopped chocolate in a medium heatproof bowl. Microwave in 30 second increments, stirring each time, until completely melted.

Add the brown and white sugar and stir to combine. Add the eggs and stir until combined.

Add the cocoa powder, flour and salt and stir until almost combined but streaks of flour are still visible. Stir in the chocolate chips/chunks until just combined.

Pour the batter into the prepared pan, smoothing the top.

Bake for about 30 minutes, until the edges are slightly puffed and the middle is set. The toothpick test won't work for these because of the fudge like texture. You can also use an instant-read thermometer to test the middle of the brownies. You would want a temperature around 180-190 degrees F.

Let the brownies cool slightly and then refrigerate them for a couple of hours to allow them to solidify and make them easier to cut.

Boston Cream Pie

Yields 10 servings

Ingredients for Custard:

3	Egg yolks, large
½ cup.	Granulated sugar
2 Tbsp.	Cornstarch
1/8 tsp.	Kosher salt
1 cup.	Whole milk
¼ cup.	Heavy cream
1 Tbsp.	Unsalted butter
1 tsp.	Pure Vanilla Extract

Ingredients for the Cake:

8 Tbsp.	Unsalted butter, cut into pieces
1¾ cups.	All-Purpose flour
1¾ tsp.	Baking powder
¾ tsp.	Kosher salt
¾ cup.	Whole milk
3	Eggs, large at room temperature
1 cup.	Granulated sugar
1 tsp.	Pure Vanilla Extract

Ingredients for the Glaze:

¼ cup.	Heavy cream
4 oz.	Semisweet chocolate chips
1 tsp.	Vegetable oil
1/8 tsp.	Kosher salt

Make the custard:

In a medium saucepan, whisk together egg yolks and sugar until well combined. Whisk in cornstarch and salt. In a slow, steady stream, whisk in milk and then the cream. Add butter. Cook mixture over medium-low heat, stirring constantly with a wooden spoon, just until it starts to thicken. Immediately whisk mixture until smooth, then continue to cook and stir custard until it has come to a very low boil for 2 minutes, about 6 to 8 minutes total. Strain custard through a fine mesh sieve into a small bowl, pushing it through with a small spatula. Stir in vanilla. Cover with plastic wrap, pressing the plastic directly onto the surface. Chill for at least 3 hours and up to 24 hours.

Prepare the cake:

Heat oven to 325 degrees. Butter a 9-by-2-inch round baking pan, generously greasing the sides, and line it with parchment paper. Butter the parchment paper as well. In a medium bowl, whisk together flour, baking powder and salt.

In a small saucepan, bring the milk and butter to a simmer over medium heat. When the butter is melted, remove pan from heat. In a large bowl, beat eggs and sugar with an electric mixer until pale and thick, about 4 to 6 minutes. With the mixer running on low, add the milk mixture and beat until combined. Then add flour mixture and vanilla and beat until combined.

Transfer to a rack and let cool 10 minutes. With a very thin knife, cut around the edge to release the cake from the side of the pan. Carefully flip the cake onto the rack, then turn it right-side-up to cool completely.

Assemble the cake:
Using a serrated knife, carefully cut the cake into two layers and place the bottom layer on a serving plate. Stir custard, and spread it onto the cut side of the bottom half. Replace the top half of the cake, cut side down.

Prepare the glaze:
In a small saucepan over medium-low, heat the cream to a simmer. Remove the pot from the heat and pour cream over the chocolate chips, oil, salt and let stand for 3 minutes. Whisk until smooth. Spread the glaze evenly over the top of the cake.

How Sweet It Is!

The catchphrase "How Sweet It Is!" has been used in a variety of ways over the decades. In the 1960s, Marvin Gaye had a hit song titled How Sweet It Is (To Be Loved By You), but perhaps its most iconic use came from comedy legend Jackie Gleason on the hit television show The Honeymooners, which cemented his and his co-stars' places in television history. I'd like to borrow this catchphrase as I share the sweet history behind the Boston Cream Pie.

I hate to be the one to break this to you, but the Boston Cream Pie isn't actually a pie at all. The history and significance of the dessert date back as far as the 1830s, when the terms "pie" and "cake" were sometimes used interchangeably (though nobody is entirely certain). The dessert is thought to have been created between 1830 and 1856, with its invention credited to French chef Augustine Francois Anezin at the Parker House Hotel in Boston, where he reportedly made it for the hotel's grand opening in 1856.

The Boston Cream Pie is considered a descendant of an earlier cake known as American Pudding Cake, Beecher's Cream Cake, or another version called Washington Pie. The dessert, originally named Parker Chocolate Cream Pie, was added to the hotel's final menu and became known as the Boston Cream Pie. The cake consists of two layers of French butter sponge cake filled with a thick custard and brushed with rum syrup. Initially, the sides of the cake were coated with the same custard, sprinkled with toasted sliced almonds, and topped with a chocolate fondant. While other custard-filled cakes may have existed at the time, the use of baking chocolate as a coating was innovative, making it unique and a popular menu choice.

As the years passed, variations of the cake began to surface, with one of the most notable being the Boston Cream Doughnut. This doughnut is made with yeast-risen dough, which is fried, and forms a cavity during frying. While still warm, the doughnut is filled with a similar cream filling and topped with a chocolate glaze. The doughnut adaptation of the cake makes it easier to eat on the go and has become a beloved treat in both the United States and Canada.

S'Mores

Ingredients:

6 large marshmallow
6 graham cracker
9 ounce chocolate bar

Yields 3 servings

Instructions:

Heat marshmallow over an open flame until it begins to brown and melt.

Break graham cracker in half; sandwich chocolate between graham cracker and hot marshmallow. Allow marshmallow to cool a little before eating.

S'More History

First recorded in 1927 in the Tramping and Trailing with the Girl Scouts as a campfire treat named "Some More" because everyone always wanted some more helpings of it. The name was then shortened to "S'more". The S'more became a ritual after a long day out in nature in with the girl scouts. Between the 1940's and the 1960's camping surged in popularity with the expansion of national parks, family road trips, and recreational camping. With this, so did the s'more. S'mores became ingrained in American outdoor heritage because they were simple, accessible and nostalgic. Unlike many desserts, s'mores aren't about perfection, they are about the experience.

Chocolate Mousse

Ingredients: Yields 8 servings

3	Eggs, Large & separated
⅓ cup.	Granulated sugar
2¼ cups.	Heavy cream, divided
7 oz.	Semi-sweet chocolate bars finely chopped

Toppings: (Optional):

Whipped cream
chocolate shavings

Instructions:

In a large bowl, whisk together egg yolks and sugar for about 1 minute, just until lightened in color and velvety.

In a small saucepan, heat 1¼ cups of cream over medium heat just until it's steaming, about 4 minutes. Remove from the heat.

Add the chocolate and stir constantly until fully melted. Slowly whisk chocolate into the egg yolks until fully combined. Set aside to cool, stirring occasionally, until barely warm to the touch, about 30 minutes.

In another large bowl, beat the egg whites until stiff peaks form. Fold a third of the egg white mixture into the chocolate mixture to loosen it. Fold the remaining egg white mixture in just until a few streaks remain.

In a large bowl, beat the remaining 1 cup of cream until stiff peaks form. Fold whipped cream into the chocolate mixture. Fill 6 to 8 small serving glasses with the mousse.

Chill until set, about 4 hours or up to 2 days. (If chilling for more than a few hours before serving, loosely cover the mousse to keep it from forming a skin and drying out.) Serve topped with whipped cream and chocolate shavings, if desired.

Did You Know.... ??

That chocolate mousse was originally knows as "mayonnaise de chocolate" Chocolate mousse was created by renowned French post impressionist painter Henri Toulouse Lautrec In the United States we celebrate National Chocolate Mousse Day on April 3rd.

Chocolate mousse was originally a savory pudding speculated to have had foie gras in it.

Bread Pudding with Caramel Bourbon Sauce

Ingredients for Bread Pudding:

6 slices.	Old bread, torn into small pieces
2 Tbsp.	Unsalted butter, melted
½ cup.	Raisins (Optional)
2 cups.	Whole milk
¾ cup.	Granulated sugar
4	Eggs, large & beaten
1 tsp.	Cinnamon, ground
1 tsp.	Vanilla extract

Ingredients For Sauce: Yields 6 servings

1 cup.	1 Granulated sugar
¼ cup.	Water
½ cup.	Heavy cream, at room temperature
¼ cup.	Butter, at room temperature
1 tsp.	Vanilla extract
2 Tbsp.	Bourbon
1 tsp.	Sea salt, fine

Instructions for Bread Pudding:

Preheat the oven to 350 degrees F.

Place bread pieces into an 8-inch square baking pan. Drizzle melted butter over bread and sprinkle raisins (optional) over top.

Whisk milk, sugar, eggs, cinnamon, and vanilla together in a medium mixing bowl until well combined.

Pour mixture over bread, and lightly push down with a fork until all bread is covered and soaking up the liquid.

Bake in the preheated oven until golden brown and the top springs back when lightly pressed, about 45 minutes.

Instructions For Sauce:

Combine the sugar and water in a heavy-bottomed sauce pan. Briefly stir to combine.

Turn the burner on to medium-high heat. Then — this is very important — do not stir or touch the pan until the sugar has caramelized. The sugar mixture will go from being completely clear, to a champagne color, to a light golden color, and then to increasingly darker shades of amber. (Keep a close eye on the sugar, as it darkens quickly once it begins to caramelize.) Once the sugar reaches a deep amber color (about the color of a copper penny), remove the saucepan from the heat and turn the burner off.

Right away, begin to slowly and carefully pour the heavy cream into the sugar mixture, whisking as you pour to quickly incorporate the cream. (The mixture will bubble furiously when the cream hits the hot sugar, so be very careful!) Add in the butter and whisk until combined. Add in the vanilla, bourbon and sea sea salt, and whisk until combined.

Serve immediately. Or let the sauce cool until it reaches room temperature (it will thicken considerably as it cools), then transfer the sauce to a sealed container and refrigerate for up to 2 weeks.

Challah French Toast

Ingredients: **Yields 6 to 8 servings**

2 cups.	Whole milk
½ cup.	Heavy cream
4	Eggs, large
2	Egg yolks, large
2 tsp.	Vanilla extract
½ tsp.	Lemon zest, finely grated (optional)
¾ tsp.	Cardamom, ground
¼ tsp.	Salt
1 loaf.	Challah bread, cut into 1¼-inch slices
6 Tbsp.	Unsalted butter
¼ cup.	Granulated sugar
½ tsp.	Cinnamon, ground

Instructions:

In a large bowl, whisk together milk, cream, eggs and egg yolks, vanilla, lemon zest (if using), ½ teaspoon cardamom and salt.

Arrange challah slices in an even layer on a rimmed baking sheet. Pour custard on top, and let sit at room temperature, uncovered, for 30 minutes, so the bread can absorb the custard, carefully flipping bread slices halfway through.

In a medium bowl, whisk together sugar, cinnamon and remaining ¼ teaspoon cardamom. Set aside.

Heat a large nonstick or cast-iron skillet over medium, then add 2 tablespoons butter and let it melt. Place 2 to 3 pieces soaked challah in skillet, making sure to not crowd the pan. Cook until golden on bottom, 4 to 5 minutes.

Sprinkle a little of the cinnamon-sugar mixture on top of each slice, then flip and cook until bottom is glazed and browned, another 4 to 5 minutes. Transfer to serving plates, glazed-side up. Repeat with remaining butter, challah and cinnamon sugar. Serve warm, with your choice of toppings.

Buttermilk Pancakes

Ingredients: **Yields 18 - 20 3 inch pancakes**

2 $^{1/2}$ cups.	All Purpose Flour
2 Tbsp.	Granulated sugar
1 $^{1/2}$ tsp.	Salt
1 tsp.	Baking powder
1 tsp.	Baking soda
2	Eggs, large & separated
2 cups.	Buttermilk
$^{1/2}$ cup.	Whole milk
10 Tbsp.	Unsalted butter, melted and cooled
As needed.	Unsalted butter for cooking

Instructions:

Heat the oven to 225°F and prepare a large baking sheet by setting a cooling rack inside. Place both in the oven.

Whisk the flour, sugar, salt, baking powder, and baking soda together in a large bowl. In a separate smaller bowl, whisk the egg yolks, buttermilk, and milk. Add the melted, cooled butter and whisk until well combined.

Pour the yolk and milk mixture into the flour mixture and stir with a wooden spoon until barely combined. Add the egg whites and stir just until a thick batter is formed. Set aside for 5 minutes.

Heat a large skillet over medium-high heat. When hot, film with $^{1/2}$ teaspoon of neutral oil such as canola or peanut oil or unsalted butter. After about 30 seconds, when the oil shimmers but is not smoking, lower the heat to medium-low and using a ladle to drop in heaping spoon fuls of pancake batter.

The batter will spread into a pancake about 3 inches wide. Cook for about 2 $^{1/2}$ minutes. (If the pancake scorches or the oil smokes, lower the heat.) When the bubbles that form on the edges of the pancakes look dry and airy, use a thin spatula to gently lift one side and peek underneath. If the pancake is golden brown, flip and cook on the other side for 2 to 2 $^{1/2}$ minutes, or until the bottom of the pancake is golden brown.

Remove from the skillet to the baking sheet in the oven. Scrape any stray crumbs or scraps out of the skillet, add a little more oil, and continue to cook the remaining batter.

Cinnamon Rolls

Ingredients for Dough:

2 3/4 CUPS.	All-Purpose Flour	
1/4 cup.	Granulated sugar	
1/2 tsp.	Salt	
3/4 cup.	Whole milk	
3 Tbsp.	Unsalted butter	
2 1/4 tsp.	Instant dry yeast	
1	Egg, large at room temperature	
1 tsp.	Pure vanilla extract	

Yields 6 - 8 servings

Ingredients for Filling:

- 3 Tbsp. — Unsalted butter, softened
- 1/3 cup. — Dark brown sugar, packed
- 1 Tbsp. — Cinnamon, ground

Ingredients for Cream Cheese Icing:

- 4 oz. — Cream cheese, softened to room temperature
- 2 Tbsp. — Unsalted butter, softened
- 2/3 cup. — Confectionary sugar

Instructions to make the dough:

Whisk the flour, sugar, and salt together in a large bowl. Set aside.

Combine the milk and butter together in a heatproof bowl. Microwave or use the stove and heat until the butter has melted and the mixture is warm to the touch (about 110°F/43°C, no higher). Whisk in the yeast until it has dissolved. Pour mixture into the dry ingredients, add the egg, and stir with a sturdy rubber spatula or wooden spoon OR use a stand mixer with a paddle attachment on medium speed. Mix until a soft dough forms.

Transfer dough to a lightly floured surface. Using floured hands, knead the dough for 3-5 minutes. You should have a smooth ball of dough. If the dough is super soft or sticky, you can add a little more flour. Place in a lightly greased bowl (I use non-stick spray), cover loosely, and let the dough rest for about 10 minutes as you get the filling ingredients ready.

Fill the rolls: After 10 minutes, roll the dough out in a 14×8-inch (36×20-cm) rectangle. Spread the softened butter on top. Mix together the cinnamon and brown sugar. Sprinkle it all over the dough. Roll up the dough to make a 14-inch log. Cut into 10-12 even rolls and arrange in a lightly greased 9- or 10-inch round cake pan, pie dish, or square baking pan.

Rise: Cover the pan with aluminum foil, plastic wrap, or a clean kitchen towel. Allow the rolls to rise in a relatively warm environment for 60-90 minutes or until double in size.

Bake the rolls: After the rolls have doubled in size, preheat the oven to 375°F (190°C). Bake for 24-27 minutes, or until lightly browned. If you notice the tops are getting too brown too quickly, loosely tent the pan with aluminum foil and continue baking. If you want to be precise about their doneness, their internal temperature taken with an instant read thermometer should be around 195-200°F (91-93°C) when done. Remove pan from the oven and place pan on a wire rack as you make the icing.

Make the icing: In a medium bowl using a handheld or stand mixer fitted with a paddle or whisk attachment, beat the cream cheese on high speed until smooth and creamy. Add the butter and beat until smooth and combined, then beat in the confectioners' sugar and vanilla until combined. Using a knife or icing spatula, spread the icing over the warm rolls and serve immediately.

Cover leftover frosted or unfrosted rolls tightly and store at room temperature for up to 2 days or in the refrigerator for up to 5 days.

1: Sweden is widely credited as the birthplace of the modern cinnamon roll known there as kanelbulle, meaning "cinnamon bun."

2: The bun was likely developed in the early 20th century, following the greater availability of luxury ingredients like sugar, flour and cinnamon after World War I.

3: The Swedish version is less sweet than the American variety and is often flavored with cardamom in addition to cinnamon.

4: Sweden celebrates Kanelbullens Dag (Cinnamon Roll Day) on October 4th, a holiday established in 1999.

5: As baking traditions spread across Europe, the idea of sweet, spiced breads evolves in various forms such as Germany's schnecken and Britain's Chelsea Buns, both of which influenced the creation of the cinnamon roll.

Churros with Chocolate Sauce

Ingredients for Churro Batter: **Yields 10 servings**

1 cup.	Water
2 ½ Tbsp.	Granulated sugar
½ tsp.	Salt
2 Tbsp.	Vegetable oil
1 cup.	All-purpose flour
2 qz.	Vegetable Oil, for frying
½ cup.	Granulated sugar, or to taste
1 tsp.	Cinnamon, ground

Ingredients for Chocolate Sauce:

¾ cup.	Granulated sugar
½ cup.	Unsweetened cocoa powder
1 ½ Tbsp.	All-purpose flour
1 ¼ cups.	Whole milk
2 Tbsp.	Unsalted butter
½ tsp.	Vanilla extract
1/8 tsp.	Salt

Instructions for Churro Dough:

Combine water, 2 ½ tablespoons sugar, salt, and 2 tablespoons vegetable oil in a small saucepan and place over medium heat.

Bring to a boil and remove from the heat.

Stir in flour, stirring until mixture forms a ball.

Heat oil for frying in a deep fryer or deep pot to 375 degrees F. Transfer dough to a sturdy pastry bag fitted with a medium star tip.

Carefully pipe a few 5- to 6-inch strips of dough into the hot oil; work in batches so you don't crowd the fryer.

Cook until golden; use a spider or slotted spoon to transfer churros to paper towels to drain.

Combine $^{1/2}$ cup sugar and cinnamon. Roll drained churros in cinnamon and sugar mixture.

Directions for Chocolate Sauce:

Place sugar, cocoa powder, and flour into a bowl. Whisk together to remove lumps.

Heat milk, butter, and vanilla extract in a saucepan over medium heat until butter melts.

Whisk dry ingredients into the milk mixture a little at a time. Increase heat to medium-high until mixture comes to a simmer.

Cook, stirring constantly, for 6 minutes, then turn off the heat. Whisk in a pinch of salt.

Chocolate Chip Cookies

Ingredients: **Yields 24 cookies**

2 cups.	All-purpose flour, spooned and leveled
1 tsp.	Baking soda
1 tsp.	Sea salt
¾ cup.	Unsalted butter, melted and cooled slightly
½ cup.	Brown sugar, packed
½ cup.	Granulated sugar
1	Egg, large
1	Egg yolk, large
2 tsp.	Vanilla extract
1 ¾ cups.	Dark chocolate chips

Instructions:

In a medium bowl, whisk together the flour, baking soda, and salt.

In a large bowl, whisk together the melted butter, brown sugar, and granulated sugar. Add the egg and egg yolk and whisk until well combined and no streaks of egg white remain. Whisk in the vanilla.

Add the dry ingredients to the wet ingredients and mix with a spatula. When the dry and wet ingredients are mostly combined, add the chocolate chips and mix until a soft cookie dough forms and no dry flour remains.

Cover and refrigerate for at least 30 minutes and up to 2 days. Cookie dough chilled for just 30 minutes will yield flatter cookies that spread more as they bake. Cookie dough chilled for 2 hours or more will yield thicker cookies that spread less.

Use a 2-tablespoon cookie scoop to scoop the dough onto the baking sheets, leaving at least 2 inches between cookies. Bake, one sheet at a time, for 9 to 11 minutes, or until the edges of the cookies are golden brown but the tops are still pale. They will look underdone when you take them out of the oven, but they will set up as they cool.

Let cool on the baking sheets for 10 minutes before transferring to a wire rack to cool completely.

A Food Reflection
A Matter of Balance

The term "guilty pleasures" often carries a negative connotation, suggesting that certain foods are "forbidden" or should be avoided. As a chef, I believe that all foods have a place at the table. Just like any other food, "guilty pleasure" items are deeply rooted in culture, history, and the comfort they provide. Indulging in these foods is essential for our mental well-being. In our fast-paced and often highly stressful lives, allowing ourselves to enjoy these foods provides a much-needed break from the pressures of daily life. Whether it's a slice of chocolate cake or a juicy hamburger, these foods undoubtedly offer various forms of satisfaction.

Guilty pleasure foods also have the ability to evoke nostalgic memories, bringing a sense of contentment and happiness. While a balanced diet is important, occasional indulgence is also part of the balance we need.

The concept of guilty pleasure foods often sparks dialogue about societal norms, pressures, and self-acceptance. While some may feel a sense of shame when indulging, it is crucial to remember that enjoying certain foods does not define our health or self-worth. In fact, allowing ourselves the freedom to savor these moments can contribute to a more balanced and disciplined relationship with food.

What we eat plays a significant role in shaping who we are. Food functions as a code, a shorthand for how we see ourselves within the communities around us. It is also intricately linked to our memories. Certain foods can trigger powerful waves of nostalgia. Though these memories can resurface at any time, we often form strong associations with food during our childhood years—those formative times when we first establish connections with the tastes and smells of our environment. All foods are links to our childhoods, the neighborhoods we grew up in, and our families. The food choices we make are shaped by these factors.

The term "guilty pleasure" is frequently used in pop culture, referring to things like television shows and music. While there's usually nothing inherently wrong with these interests, the term takes on a different tone when applied to food. We are already bombarded with mixed messages about how we should eat, and the use of terms like "guilty pleasure" only adds to the pressure, shaping how we feel about what we eat. In pop culture, "guilty pleasure" refers to something someone enjoys that others deem unworthy of praise or subpar.

The shame that people often feel, imposed by others or themselves, can create a negative emotional response. This stress can lead to emotional eating, which can spiral into unhealthy patterns. The words we use to describe food have a profound impact on our beliefs and our relationship with it. There is no such thing as "bad" or "good" food—only food that serves different purposes in our lives.

Pistachio Layer Cake

Ingredients for Cake: **Yields 8 servings**

1 cup.	Unsalted butter
3 cups.	Cake flour
2 cups.	Granulated sugar
1 tsp.	Baking powder
½ tsp.	Baking soda
¾ tsp.	Salt
1 ½ cups.	Buttermilk room temperature
2	Eggs, large room temperature
½ tsp.	Vanilla Extract
¾ tsp.	Almond extract
1 cup.	Pistachios, dry roasted finely chopped

Ingredients for Swiss Meringue Buttercream:

6 large.	Egg whites
1 ¾ cups.	Granulated sugar
¼ tsp.	Salt
2 cups.	Unsalted butter, Room temperature
1 ½ tsp.	Vanilla Extract

Instructions for Cake:

Melt butter in a medium sized saucepan over medium heat.

Decrease heat to medium-low and cook, stirring and scraping the bottom with a heatproof spatula, until brown bits form on the bottom of the pan (the butter will sizzle, foam, and pop then this will slow down just before it browns). Pour into a heatproof bowl and allow to cool until no longer warm to the touch before proceeding.

Preheat oven to 350F and grease 3- 8" round baking pans with baking spray. Line the bottoms with rounds of parchment paper to ensure the cakes won't stick.

In a large mixing bowl (or the bowl of a stand mixer), whisk together cake flour, sugar, baking powder, baking soda, and salt.

Add the cooled browned butter and use an electric mixer to stir on low-speed until thoroughly incorporated.

In a separate, medium-sized, whisk together buttermilk, eggs, and extracts until well-combined.

With mixer on low-speed, gradually drizzle the buttermilk mixture into the flour mixture. Scrape the sides and bottom of the bowl to ensure the batter is uniform (it's alright if you notice small lumps in the batter).

Add pistachios and use a spatula to stir until well incorporated.

Add drops of green food coloring, if desired. Stir until uniform in color.

Evenly divide batter into prepared pans and bake in the center rack of 350F oven for 25 minutes or until a toothpick inserted in the center comes out clean or with moist crumbs.

Allow cakes to cool in their pans for 15 minutes before running a knife around the edge of the cake to loosen it from the pan then carefully invert onto a cooling rack to cool completely. Cakes must be completely cooled before decorating.

Instruction for Swiss Merigue Buttercream:

In clean, dry mixer bowl, combine egg whites, sugar, and salt and whisk until combined.

Heat about 1 ½ inches of water over medium-low heat in a medium-sized saucepan and bring to a simmer.

Rest the bowl of your mixer in the pot over the simmering water (it should not be touching the water).

Whisk egg white mixture constantly until the sugar is dissolved and mixture is no longer grainy (if you rub a small bit between your fingers it should feel smooth and not at all gritty) and the mixture reaches 160F. This will take several minutes.

Remove mixing bowl from heat and dry the bottom of your bowl. Fit bowl into your stand mixer.

Using a whisk attachment, beat the egg whites on medium/medium-high speed until meringue is thick and glossy and you have achieved stiff peaks. This will take about 10 minutes.

Once you have achieved stiff peaks, stop beating and allow bowl to cool down completely. The bowl must no longer be warm to the touch before proceeding.

Once bowl is no longer warm to the touch (make sure you are feeling near the bottom of the bowl), switch out whisk attachment for paddle attachment. Turn mixer to medium speed and add butter one tablespoon at a time. Don't add the next tablespoon of butter until the previous one is incorporated into the meringue. If you notice that your buttercream starts to break down or look curdled, just keep mixing and it will come together. If it still doesn't come together (it could take some time), place the mixer bowl in the fridge for about 10 minutes and then try mixing again.

Once all butter has been beaten into the meringue, scrape down the sides of the bowl and stir again. Beat on medium/high until smooth and thick. Stir in vanilla extract or other flavoring and any food coloring, if using.

Once the meringue is complete, place the first layer of cake on your serving plate, cake board or cake pedestal. Center the cake onto the surface. To ensure that the cake is level, the bottom of each cake should be the top. Invert the cakes so the flat and even bottoms become the top of each level of the cake. Spread a small amount of the the prepared meringue onto the first later of the cake evenly. Add the second layer of cake, and once again spread a small amount of the merit topping the second layer of cake and lastly place the third and final layer of cake on top of the second layer of filling. At this point you should have three layers of cake and two layers of filling. At this point the cake is assembled.

Using an offset spatula if you have one, start spreading the meringue on the outside of the cake to make a thin and even coat of buttercream. Once the sides are done, you can now frost the top of the cake until fully covered. The offset spatula is useful because it will aid in evenly distributing the meringue as well as maneuvering the buttercream as you apply it.

Once the cake is completely covered in buttercream allow to sit in the refrigerator for 2 hours to settle..

Dutch Apple Pie

Yields 10 servings

Ingredients For the Pie Crust:

1 1/4 cups.	All-Purpose Flour
1/2 tsp.	Kosher salt
1/4 cup.	Unsalted butter, cold
2 1/2 Tbsp.	Vegetable oil
1/4 cup.	Ice water

For the Apple Pie Filling:

10	Apples, Granny Smith and Honey Belt
1/2 cup.	Granulated sugar
3 Tbsp.	All-purpose flour
2 Tbsp.	Lemon juice
2 1/2 tsp.	Cinnamon, ground
1/2 tsp.	Nutmeg, ground
1/4 tsp.	Kosher salt
1/8 tsp.	Cloves, ground

For the Crumb Topping:

8 Tbsp.	Unsalted butter
1 1/2 cups.	All-purpose flour
1/2 cup.	Light brown sugar
1 tsp.	Cinnamon, ground
1/4 tsp.	Kosher salt

Instructions To Make the Pie Crust:

Place the flour and salt in a large bowl, and whisk to combine. Add the oil, stirring until the mixture resembles coarse crumbs. Cut the butter into thin slices and toss in the flour mixture to coat. Drizzle ice water in, one tablespoon at a time, mixing just until the mixture can hold its shape. (You may need slightly more or less water.) Remove the dough out of the bowl and onto a large sheet of plastic wrap. Use the plastic wrap to gather the dough into a disc shape, then wrap the dough tightly and press down on it firmly to compact it. Chill the dough in the refrigerator for 1 hour. Flour the work surface, rolling pin, and the chilled dough lightly, then roll out to 1/4-inch thickness, and fold into thirds. Give it a quarter-turn, fold into thirds again, then repeat one more time. Refrigerate for one more hour, Roll out the pie crust dough to a little larger than the width of your pie pan and gently nestle it in, allowing any excess to drape over the sides. Trim, fold under, and crimp the edge, then chill.

To Make the Apple Pie Filling:

Peel, quarter, and cut out the cores of the apples. Cut into 1/8-inch to 1/4-inch thick slices. Toss together in a large bowl with sugar, flour, lemon juice, cinnamon, nutmeg, salt, and cloves. Transfer the filling to the prepared pie shell and chill for one hour.

To Make the Crumb Topping:

Melt the butter in a small pot, then add flour, brown sugar, cinnamon, and salt. Toss together with a fork and sprinkle over the top of the pie.

To Bake the Dutch Apple Pie:

Preheat the oven to 400 degrees F. Bake the pie until the apples feel softened and tender when pierced with a toothpick, but not mushy (approx. 55 to 70 minutes).Cool completely and dust with powdered sugar before slicing.

Lemon Bars

Ingredients for Crust:　　　　　　　　　　　　　　　　　　　　　　　　　**Yields 12 servings**

1 cup.	Unsalted butter, room temperature
½ cup.	Granulated sugar
2 cups.	All-Purpose Flour

Ingredients for Filling:

4	Eggs, large at room temperature
1 ½ cups.	Granulated sugar
¼ cup.	All-Purpose Flour
⅔ cup.	Lemon juice

Instructions for Crust:

Preheat oven to 350°F.

In a medium bowl, blend together softened butter, 2 cups flour, and ½ cup sugar with a pastry cutter, a fork, or your hands. Press into the bottom of a 9x13 inch pan lined with parchment paper. Bake for 15-20 minutes in the preheated oven, or until firm and golden.

Instructions for Filling:

Whisk together 1 ½ cups sugar and ¼ cup flour. Crack eggs into a separate bowl, then whisk them into the sugar and flour mixture. Add ⅔ cup lemon juice and mix until well combined. Pour over the baked crust.
Bake uncovered for an additional 20 minutes in the oven. Allow bars to cool in the refrigerator for at least 2 hours then dust with confectioners sugar. Cut into squares and serve.

Coconut Layer Cake

Yields 8 servings

Ingredients for Cake:

2 1/2 cups.	Cake Flour
2 tsp.	Baking powder
1/2 tsp.	Baking soda
1 tsp.	Salt
3/4 cup.	Unsalted butter, room temperature
1 2/3 cups.	Granulated sugar
5	Egg whites, large at room temperature
1/2 cup.	Sour cream, at room temperature
2 tsp.	Pure Vanilla Extract
1 tsp.	Coconut Extract
1 cup.	Unsweetened Coconut Milk, room temperature
1 cup.	Sweetened shredded coconut

Ingredients for Coconut Cream Cheese Buttercream:

1 cup	Unsalted butter, softened
8 oz.	Cream cheese, softened to room temperature
5 cups.	Confectioners sugar
2 Tbsp.	Coconut Milk, canned
1/2 tsp.	Pure Vanilla extract
1/2 tsp.	Coconut Extract
1/8 tsp.	Salt
2 cups.	Sweetened shredded coconut

Instructions for Cake:

Preheat oven to 350°F. Grease three 9-inch cake pans, line with parchment paper rounds, then grease the parchment paper. Parchment paper helps the cakes seamlessly release from the pans.

Instructions for Make the cake:

Whisk the cake flour, baking powder, baking soda, and salt together. Set aside.

Using a handheld or stand mixer fitted with a paddle or whisk attachment, beat the butter and sugar together on medium-high speed until smooth and creamy, about 2 minutes. Scrape down the sides and up the bottom of the bowl with a rubber spatula as needed.

Beat in the egg whites until combined, then add the sour cream, vanilla extract, and coconut extract. Beat until combined. Mixture will look curdled as a result of the varying textures and solid butter combining. Scrape down the sides and up the bottom of the bowl as needed. With the mixer on low speed, slowly add the dry ingredients and coconut milk. Beat on low speed until combined, then add the shredded coconut. Whisk it all by hand to make sure there are no butter lumps at the bottom of the bowl. The batter will be slightly thick.

Pour batter evenly into cake pans. Bake for 21-23 minutes or until the cakes are baked through. To test for doneness, insert a toothpick into the center of the cake. If it comes out clean, it's done. Allow cakes to cool completely in the pans set on a wire rack. The cakes must be completely cool before frosting and assembling.

Instructions for Make the Frosting:
In a large bowl using a handheld or stand mixer fitted with a whisk or paddle attachment, beat the butter and cream cheese together on medium speed until creamy and smooth, about 2 minutes. Add confectioners' sugar, coconut milk, vanilla extract, coconut extract, and salt with the mixer running on low. Increase to high speed and beat for 3 minutes. Add more confectioners' sugar if frosting is too thin, more coconut milk if frosting is too thick, or an extra pinch of salt if frosting is too sweet.

Instructions for Assemble and Decorate:
Using a large serrated knife, slice a thin layer off the tops of the cakes to create a flat surface. Place 1 cake layer on your cake board, or serving plate. Evenly cover the top with about 1 and $^{1/2}$ cups of frosting. Top with second cake layer and evenly cover the top with about 1 and $^{1/2}$ cups of frosting. Top with the third cake layer. And continue to alternate layers of frosting and cake until it is all used. Spread the remaining frosting all over the top and sides. I use and recommend an icing spatula to apply the frosting and a bench scraper to smooth the sides. Sprinkle coconut on top of the cake and apply it to the sides.

Refrigerate cake for at least 20 minutes before slicing. This helps the cake hold its shape when cutting.

All Butter Pound Cake

Ingredients for Cake: **Yields 8 servings**

3 cups.	All-Purpose Flour
1 tsp.	Baking powder
1/2 tsp.	Salt
1 cup.	Unsalted butter, room temperature
1/2 cup.	Shortening
3 cups.	Granulated sugar
5	Eggs, large at room temperature
2	Egg yolks, room temperature
1 tsp.	Vanilla Extract
1/2 tsp.	Lemon Extract
1/2 cup.	Whole Milk room temperature
1/2 cup.	Buttermilk room temperature

Instructions :

Preheat oven to 325 F.

Grease and flour a bundtpan. Set aside. In a large bowl whisk together flour, baking powder, and salt. Set aside. In a large bowl cream together butter, shortening, and sugar. Mix in eggs, one at a time, mixing thoroughly after each egg.

Mix in egg yolks. Mix in vanilla extract, lemon extract.

Add dry ingredients into wet ingredients, alternating with the milk and butter milk. Mix until batter is fluffy.

Spoon batter into prepared pan and shake the pan to even out the top and release any air bubbles.

Bake for 1 hour and test it to see if it is baked, if not bake for an additional 20 minutes, but checking frequently.

Remove from oven and let the cake sit in the pan for about 10 minutes.

Then remove from pan and place on a cooling rack to finish cooling.

Banana Cream Pie

Ingredients: **Yields 8 servings**

10 Tbsp.	Salted butter, melted
2 ⅔ cups.	Vanilla wafers or Graham crackers
5	Bananas
2	Eggs, large & at room temperature
2	Egg yolks, large & at room temperature
4 Tbsp.	Cornstarch
½ cup.	Sugar
1 tsp.	Vanilla Extract
⅛ tsp.	Sea salt
1 cup.	Heavy cream
1 cup.	Whole milk

Ingredients for Topping:

1 ½ cups.	Heavy cream
2 Tbsp.	Confectionary sugar
¼ tsp.	Vanilla extract
As needed.	Dark chocolate, shaved for garnish

Instructions for Crust:

Preheat the oven to 275°F. Choose an 8-inch or 9-inch tart pan with a removable bottom (false-bottom pan) or a regular pie tin. Lightly coat the bottom and sides with cooking spray or grease with butter.

Use a food processor or a sealable kitchen bag and a rolling pin to crush the wafers into fine crumbs.

Melt the butter and pour it into a mixing bowl or bag with the crushed wafers. Stir until the crumbs are moistened.

Press the crumb mixture firmly and evenly into the bottom and sides of the tart or pie pan using your fingers. To pack the crumbs down even more and create a smooth crust, use a tall glass or measuring cup to press the mixture inside the pan. To help prevent the crust from crumbling later, run a spoon along the edge where the bottom and sides meet to smooth out any bumps and create a rounded edge.

Instructions for Custard:

In a medium mixing bowl, whisk together the eggs, egg yolks, sugar, cornstarch, salt, and vanilla until everything is well blended and smooth.

In a small saucepan, heat 1 cup of cream and 1 cup of milk over medium heat until it gently simmers.

While continuously whisking the egg mixture in the bowl, slowly drizzle in a small amount of the hot cream and milk mixture. Keep whisking as you gradually add more of the hot liquid until everything is combined. Now, carefully pour all the contents of the bowl back into the saucepan.

Turn the heat to low and cook, while whisking, until the custard thickens to the consistency of runny pudding, about 5 minutes.

Instructions to Bake:

Thinly slice two bananas and line the bottom of the crust. Pour the warm custard over the bananas, letting it settle around them naturally. You can gently shake the pan to help the custard fill any gaps.

Place the pie in the preheated oven and bake for 30 minutes. When gently nudging the pan, the custard should be slightly unset in the center. Don't worry if you see a few cracks on top, that's normal.

Let the pie cool completely at room temperature. Then, cover the pan loosely with plastic wrap or foil and refrigerate it overnight.

Instructions to Finish the Pie:

If using a tart pan remove the pie from the tart pan and place onto a serving platter.

Use a stand mixer or an electric hand mixer to beat 1 ½ cups of heavy cream with the powdered sugar and vanilla until the medium peaks. Slice two more bananas and cover the top of the pie with them. Cover the bananas with the whipped cream, swirling it to create height. Use a fine grater or a vegetable peeler to shave dark chocolate on top.

Italian Cream Puffs with Cannoli Cream

Ingredients For the Cream Puffs: **Yields 12 Cream Puffs**

1 cup.	Water
½ cup.	Unsalted butter
½ tsp.	Granulated sugar
¼ tsp.	Kosher salt
1 cup.	All-purpose flour
4	Eggs, large

Ingredients for Cannoli Cream Filling:

16 oz.	Whole milk ricotta
8 oz.	Mascarpone
½ cup.	Super fine granulated
2 tsp.	Lemon zest
1 tsp.	Vanilla extract
½ cup.	Miniature chocolate chips

Instructions To Make the Choux Pastry Puffs:

Preheat the oven to 425 degrees F and line baking sheets with parchment paper.

Place the water, butter, sugar, and salt in a small pot and cook over medium-high heat until the butter is completely melted and the mixture is simmering.

Add in the flour all at once, and continue to cook, whisking, for about 5 minutes, or until the dough gathers itself into a ball and a film begins to form on the bottom of the pot.

Transfer the mixture to a mixing bowl, and beat on medium speed.

Drop in the eggs, one at a time, while continuing to beat. (Allow each egg to become fully incorporated before adding the next.)

Pipe or spoon the dough in 1 ½-inch balls onto the prepared baking sheets, allowing about 3 inches in between each puff.

Bake for 35 to 45 minutes, or until puffed, golden brown, hollow, dry, and light.

Allow the pastries to cool completely, then slice open horizontally or make a hole in the bottom of the cream puff, and stuff with cannoli cream filling, and dust with powdered sugar.

Instructions for Cannoli Cream Filling:

Using an electric mixer, whip the mascarpone in a large bowl until creamy (1-2 minutes).

Add the ricotta cheese, superfine granulated sugar, lemon zest (or orange zest), and vanilla extract to the mascarpone Mix by hand until well combined. Don't over mix.

Fold the mini chocolate chips into the ricotta mixture, mixing just enough to combine.

Sweet History Of The Cream Puff

The cream puff in its raw state is made from what is called choux pastry dough that was first invented in the 16th century by Panterelli a chef to Catherine de'Medici, who is credited to bringing many Italian culinary traditions to the French court when she was married to King Henry II.

Over time, the dough was refined by French chefs and eventually became known as pâte à choux with a literal translation meaning "cabbage dough" due to the shape of puffs resembling small cabbages.

Choux pastry is unique because it puffs up without any leavening agents like yeast or baking powder, it is the steam inside the dough that causes it to rise.

The cream puff are closely related to other choux based pastries like the éclair, gougères, Paris Brest, and Saint Joseph pastry.

Creme Brulee

Ingredients: **Yields 8 servings**

5	Egg yolks, large
3/4 cup.	Granulated sugar, divided
3 cups.	Heavy cream
1/4 tsp.	Salt
1 1/2 tsp.	Pure vanilla extract*

Instructions:

Preheat oven to 325°F.

Whisk the egg yolks and 1/2 cup of granulated sugar together. Set aside. (At this point or before you temper the egg yolks in the next step, bring a small kettle or pot of water to a boil. You'll need hot water to pour into the baking sheet for the water bath.)

Heat the heavy cream, and salt together in a medium saucepan over medium heat. As soon as it begins to simmer, remove from heat. Stir in the vanilla extract. Remove about 1/2 cup of warm heavy cream and, in a slow and steady stream, whisk into the egg yolks. Keep those egg yolks moving so they don't scramble. In a slow and steady stream, pour and whisk the egg yolk mixture into the warm heavy cream.

Place ramekins in a large baking pan. If you don't have 1 pan large enough, bake them in a couple pans. Divide custard between each ramekin, filling to the top. Carefully fill the pan with about a 1/2 inch of the hot water.

Bake until the edges are set and centers are a little unset. The time depends on the depth of your ramekins. Ramekins that are 1-inch deep, the custard takes 35 minutes. Begin checking them at 30 minutes. For a more accurate sign, they're done when an instant read thermometer registers 170°F.

Remove pan from the oven and, using an oven mitt, remove the ramekins from the pan. Place on a wire rack to cool for at least 1 hour. Place in the refrigerator, loosely covered, and chill for at least 4 hours and up to 2 days before topping.

Using the remaining granulated sugar, sprinkle a thin layer all over the surface of the chilled custards. Caramelize the sugar with a kitchen torch and serve immediately or store in the refrigerator for up to 1 hour before serving. Caramelized topping is best enjoyed right away.

Tarte Tatin

Ingredients: **Yields 6 servings**

1	Puff pastry sheet
¼ cup.	Salted butter
¼ cup.	Granulated sugar
4	Apples, peeled, cored and quartered

Instructions:

Preheat oven to 425 degrees F.

On a lightly floured surface, roll puff pastry and trim to fit the size of the pan you will be using for the tart. Wrap in plastic wrap and refrigerate until ready to use.

Heat pan over medium heat and melt the butter. Sprinkle the sugar evenly over the melted butter and cook, stirring occasionally until the mixture is a pale amber color. Remove pan from heat. Place apple quarters in the pan, on their sides, laying from the outer edge in. Fit in as many as possible.

Set pan to medium heat and cook until the apples become golden brown (10 minutes or so). Feel free to lift one out of the pan to check its color. Flip over each apple so the cooked edge faces up and the uncooked edge is face down in the caramel. Continue to cook until the caramel that bubbles up between the apples pieces is dark amber (8-10 more minutes).

Grab trimmed puff pastry from the refrigerator. Cut 4 slits in the pastry to allow steam to escape. Remove pan from stovetop and lay pastry over apples. Place into preheated oven and bake 20 minutes, or until pastry is golden brown.

Carefully remove pan from oven and immediately invert onto a cooling rack. If desired, place a baking sheet under the cooling rack to catch any drippings.

Serve warm or at room temperature.

Lemon Meringue Pie

Ingredients for Pie Crust:

2 1/2 cups.	All-Purpose Flour
1 tsp.	Salt
6 Tbsp.	Unsalted butter, chilled and cubed
2/3 cup.	Vegetable shortening, chilled
1/2 cup.	Ice cold water

Ingredients for Lemon Filling:

5	Egg yolks, large
1 1/3 cups.	Water
1 cup.	Granulated sugar
1/3 cup.	Cornstarch
1/4 tsp.	Salt
1/2 cup.	Lemon juice
1 Tsp.	Lemon zest

Yields 8 servings

2 Tbsp.	Unsalted butter, softened

Ingredients for Meringue:

5	Egg whites, large & at room temperature
1/2 tsp.	Cream of tartar
1/2 cup.	Granulated sugar
1/8 tsp.	Salt

Instructions for Pie Dough:

Whisk the flour and salt together in a large bowl.

Add the butter and shortening. Using a pastry cutter or two forks, cut the butter and shortening into the mixture until it resembles coarse meal (pea-sized bits with a few larger bits of fat). In this step, you're only breaking up the cold fat into tiny little flour-coated pieces; you're not completely incorporating it. Do not overwork the ingredients.

Measure 1/2 cup of water in a cup. Add ice. Stir it around. From that, measure 1/2 cup of water, since the ice has melted a bit. Drizzle the cold water in, 1 tablespoon at a time, and stir with a rubber spatula or wooden spoon after every tablespoon has been added. Stop adding water when the dough begins to form large clumps. Do not add any more water than you need.

Transfer the pie dough to a floured work surface. Using floured hands, fold the dough into itself until the flour is fully incorporated into the fats. The dough should come together easily and should not feel overly sticky. Avoid overworking the dough. If it feels a bit too dry or crumbly, dip your fingers in the ice water and then continue bringing dough together with your hands. If it feels too sticky, sprinkle on more flour and then continue bringing dough together with your hands. Form it into a ball. Use a sharp knife to cut it in half. If it's helpful, you should have about 1 lb, 8 ounces dough total. Gently flatten each half into 1-inch-thick discs using your hands.

Wrap each tightly in plastic wrap. Refrigerate for at least 2 hours and up to 5 days.

After the dough has chilled for at least 2 hours, you can roll it out. Work with one crust at a time, keeping the other in the refrigerator until you're ready to roll it out. Lightly flour the work surface, rolling pin, and your hands, and sprinkle a little flour on top of the dough. Use gentle-medium force with your rolling pin on the dough—don't press down too hard on the dough. When rolling dough out, start from the center and work your way out in all directions, turning the dough with your hands as you go. Between passes of the rolling pin, rotate the pie crust and even flip it, to make sure it's not sticking to your work surface. Sprinkle on a little more flour if it's sticking; don't be afraid to use a little more flour. If you notice the dough becoming a lopsided circle as you're rolling it out, put down the rolling pin and use your hands to help mold the dough back into an even circle. Roll the dough into a very thin 12-inch circle, which is the perfect size to fit a 9-inch pie dish. Your pie dough will be about 1/8 inch thick, which is quite thin. Visible specks of butter and fat in the dough are perfectly normal and expected.

Because your dough is so thin, use your rolling pin to help transfer the pie crust to the pie dish. Carefully roll one end of the circle of dough gently onto the rolling pin, rolling it back towards you, slowly peeling it off the work surface as you go. Pick it up, and carefully roll it back out over the top of the pie dish.

Bake in a preheated 350 degree F oven until golden brown and allow to fully cool prior to filling the crust with lemon filling.

Instructions to Make Filling:

Whisk the egg yolks together in a medium bowl or liquid measuring cup. Set aside. Whisk the water, granulated sugar, cornstarch, salt, lemon juice, and lemon zest together in a medium saucepan over medium heat. The mixture will be thin and cloudy, then eventually begin thickening and bubbling after about 6 minutes. Once thickened, give it a whisk and reduce heat to a low flame.

Temper the egg yolks:

Very slowly stream a few large spoonfuls of warm lemon mixture into the beaten egg yolks. Then, also in a very slow stream, whisk the egg yolk mixture into the saucepan. Turn heat back up to medium. Cook until the mixture is thick and big bubbles begin bursting at the surface. Remove the pan from heat and whisk in the butter. Spread filling into the warm partially baked crust. Set aside as you prepare the meringue. Don't let the filling cool down too much as you want a warm filling when you top with the meringue.

Instructions for Meringue:

With a handheld mixer or a stand mixer fitted with a whisk attachment, beat the egg whites and cream of tartar together on medium speed for 1 minute, then increase to high speed until soft peaks form, about 4 more minutes. Add the sugar and salt, then continue beating on high speed until glossy stiff peaks form, about 2 more minutes.

Spread meringue on top of filling. Make sure you spread the meringue all the way to the edges so that it touches the crust. This helps prevent the meringue from weeping.

Instructions to Finish:

Once the meringue is applied using a small kitchen torch brown the meringue from a safe distance making sure to use even application of heat to prevent dark spots over the top of the meringue.

Tiramisu

Ingredients For the Coffee Dip: **Yields 8 servings**

1 1/2 cups.	Strong black coffee or Italian Espresso
1/4 cup	Marsala wine or rum

For the Zabaione Filling:

4	Eggs, large
1/2 cup.	Granulated sugar
16 oz.	Mascarpone cheese

For the Layers:

8 oz.	Ladyfingers cookies
2 Tbsp.	Marsala wine or dark Rum
6 Tbsp.	Cocoa powder, unsweetened

Instructions:

To begin, take out the Mascarpone cheese and the eggs from the refrigerator and leave them at room temperature for about 10 minutes (use a mascarpone mixture in place of whipped cream or heavy cream for a more authentic texture flavor).

In the meantime, prepare the espresso or coffee. Once ready, pour into a shallow bowl or into a bowl large enough to be able to lay a ladyfinger cookie fully. Add the marsala or rum to the coffee or espresso and mix.

Then, using two medium-large mixing bowls, separate the egg whites from the raw egg yolks. In the mixing bowl with the egg yolks, combine the yolks and sugar and whip the yolks with a kitchen mixer or an electric hand mixer until the mixture becomes creamy.

Add the Mascarpone cheese to the egg yolk mixture and, with the help of a spatula, mix gently until all the ingredients have been incorporated.

In the second mixing bowl with the egg whites, whip the egg whites to form stiff peaks using an electric hand mixer or a stand mixer. Then, with a spatula, take a bit of the stiff peaks of the egg white mixture and fold slowly into the yolk mixture. Gently bring the egg mixture up and turn it over back into the bowl.

Repeat this folding action turning the bowl a bit as you go until the egg white mixture is fully incorporated and the resulting mixture is light and airy.

Cover the bottom of your baking dish with a layer of the cream mixture.

Now is the time to quickly dip a couple of lady fingers in the bowl with the coffee. Dip both sides of the cookie. This action should be quick enough to avoid soaking the cookies too much. If it's your first time, start with just one lady finger first before proceeding with the others to get a sense of the timing.

Lay the coffee-soaked lady fingers on top of the first layer of the mixture in the baking pan. Repeat until the cookies cover the mixture entirely. Do not overlap the cookies.

Spread another layer of the mixture on top of the cookies.

Lay another layer of coffee-dipped lady fingers and cover the cookies with another layer of the mixture. Level the mixture with the spatula.

Place the tiramisu in the fridge for at least 3 hours. Before serving, dust with cocoa powder. To do this, use a fine strainer sprinkle the cocoa powder on top of the tiramisu cake, and serve.

Peach Cobbler

Ingredients: **Yields 6 servings**

7	Peaches, thinly sliced
1 ½ tsp.	Lemon juice
¾ cup.	All Purpose Flour
¼ cup.	Granulated sugar
¼ tsp.	Cinnamon, ground
¼ tsp.	Baking soda
¼ tsp.	Salt
¼ cup.	Unsalted butter
1 tsp.	Vanilla extract

Instructions:

Preheat the oven to 400°F and grease a 9x13-inch baking dish with melted unsalted butter.

Layer the peaches into the bottom of the baking dish and drizzle the lemon juice over the peaches.

In a medium bowl, mix the flour, sugar, cinnamon, baking soda, and salt. Add the unsalted butter and vanilla and combine until the mixture forms a crumbly dough. Sprinkle over the peaches and bake for 30 minutes, or until the mixture is just lightly browned on top and the peaches are juicy.

Inventing The Cobbler...

As early as the 1700's English colonists, tried to recreate familiar British puddings and pies. Lacking proper ovens and ingredients on the frontier, they adapted by stewing fruit and spooning over a silly dough or batter over it before baking it over open fires or in hearths. The dish was easier to make with limited resources and it used seasonal fruits that were available making the dish very versatile. Cobbler received its name because after cooking the top of the dessert resembled stones in a cobblestone street. Because of it's British background, cobblers are considered the culinary cousin of Crumbles, Brown Betty's and Eve Pudding. The Georgia Peach Council named April 13th as National Peach Cobbler Day.

Rice Pudding

Ingredients: **Yields 8 servings**

4 cups.	Whole milk
As needed.	Whole milk
1/2 cup.	Long grain white rice
2/3 cup.	Heavy cream
1/3 cup.	Granulated sugar
2	Egg yolks, large
1 1/2 tsp.	Pure vanilla extract
1/8 tsp.	Salt
1/2 cup.	Raisins, optional

Instructions:

Rinse a large saucepan with cold water. Don't dry. Set on stove-top over medium heat. Add 4 cups whole milk. Heat milk to boiling, over medium heat, stirring regularly. Watch closely as it nears the boil! When milk hits the boil, it will boil up and possibly over the pot.

When milk boils, stir in rice and keep stirring until mixture returns to the boil. Reduce heat to a slightly higher than low, or whatever level on your stove allows the mixture to gently simmer (bubble breaking the surface but not too vigorously). Simmer for 30 minutes, stirring down the mixture every 10 minutes (Important that you stir it down regularly and ensure that there is no rice sticking to the bottom of the pan. You will notice that the mixture has probably formed a skin on top. Don't remove it. Just stir it back in.)

Meanwhile, in a medium-sized bowl, use a fork to whisk together the cream, sugar, yolks, vanilla and salt. Set aside on counter while rice is cooking, leaving fork in bowl. Set out a ladle to use, as well.

Once milk/rice has simmered for 30 minutes, continue simmering, but stir down every 5 minutes. With each stir, start testing the done-ness of the rice by tasting a piece. You want the rice to be tender. Depending on the rice you used, your mixture may start to get thick at this point, with little milky liquid left. If so, add more hot milk or water to the pot, just as much as needed to loosen the mixture up, with each stir. Watch closely and don't let the mixture get dry or it will burn. Continue cooking, stirring down and adding additional milk, as needed until the rice is tender. Most rice is generally done at about 45-50 minutes of total simmering time. A lot will depend on how vigorously your mixture is boiling, so there is no hard and fast rule. Taste testing is the best indicator.

Once the rice is cooked, slide the pot off the heat to avoid scorching. Re-whisk your egg mixture with your fork. Using the ladle, spoon out a ladle-full of hot rice/milk mixture, taking as much liquid as possible, but not to worry if you bring some of the rice with it. With the ladle start adding the hot mixture to the eggs slowly to temper the eggs at first, while continuously whisking with the fork. Increase to a slow stream, while whisking continuously, until the entire ladle-full has been added. Get another ladle full of hot liquid and slowly add it to the egg mixture as well, whisking continuously. Keep adding hot liquid until you've got at least 1 1/2 cups-1 3/4 cups of now warmed liquid in your bowl. Once you have reached that point, pour the warmed egg mixture into your cooking pot.

Return the saucepan to heat, over medium-low heat. Cook, stirring almost continuously, just until a dime-sized bubble breaks the surface of the pudding. Pudding should be noticeably thickened and saucy, but still more sauce than rice (pudding will set more in the refrigerator as it cools). If liquid seems almost like milk consistency (rather than heavy cream consistency), it's too thin. Cook, stirring, a little longer. Note though that you never want to allow the mixture to vigorously boil after the egg mixture has been added, as you may end up with scrambled eggs.

If using raisins, add to the bottom of a medium-large bowl. When pudding is cooked, immediately pour hot mixture over raisins. Stir well to combine. Allow to stand on counter for about 5 minutes, to allow the steam to reduce, then cover bowl with plastic wrap and place into the refrigerator. Allow to cool and set, at least 6 hours or preferably, over-night. Pudding will set as it cools. To serve, simply stir and spoon into bowls. Serve with a sprinkling of cinnamon, if desired. If pudding is or becomes too thick, simply add a tablespoon or so of heavy cream to mixture and stir in.

Global Rice Pudding!

Rice pudding like many guilty pleasure foods have traveled around the world! Various cultures have their own version of it. In India, Kheer is made with basmati rice, cardamom, saffron and sometimes nuts and raisins. In Spain and Latin America known as Arroz Con Leche often flavored with cinnamon, lemon or orange zest. In the Middle East, known as Roz Bel Laban, flavored with rosewater or orange blossom. In Nordic countries known as Risgrynsgröt or Risalamande served only during Christmas time usually with almonds and cream. In the United Kingdom it is baked in the oven or on the stove top seasoned with freshly grated nutmeg or fresh jam. Rice pudding gained popularity as a way of using left over rice or milk during wartime and the Depression and continued to be a staple in cultures all around the world thereafter.

Index

A
Alenis Soyer, 60
Apple, 99
Augustine Anezin, 81

B
Bacon, 81
Banana, 107
Basil, 25,35,48,50,64
Beans, 26,39,57,67
Beef, ground chuck, 67,68
Belgium, 23,60
Belgium waffles, 23
Bensonhurst, 33
Biscuits, 42
Boston, 15,33,79,81
Bourbon, 84
Breadcrumbs, 48
Brine, 23-24,
Brooklyn, 33-34
Brownies, 78,
Buttercream, 74,96,97.98,103
Buttermilk, 23,88,96

C
Cake, 96
Cannoli, 110
Caramel,84
Cayenne, 39
Challah bread, 86
Charles Dickens, 60
Cheese, 21,26-27,53,65,76
Cheese, American, Cheddar, Gruyere, Ricotta, Mozzarella, 21,25,33,65
Chicken, nuggets, thighs, breast, wings, 23,48,56,64
Chocolate, 82,90,92
Chowder, 54
Churro, 91
Cilantro, 57

Cinnamon, 89
Clams, 54
Cobbler, 119
Coconut, 103
Cod, 59
Cookies, 93
Corn, 41,57
Corn Dogs, 41
Cornmeal, 62
Cream cheese, 65,76,89,103
Cream puffs, 110
Creme Brûlée, 112
Cumi, 112
Cupcakes, 74

D
Dominos, 34
Dough, 35, 65,89

E
Espresso, 117

F
French fries, 26,27,32,59,72
French toast, 86
Fries, 26-27

H
Ham, 29
Hamburger, 29,95
Honey, 23-24
Hot Dogs, 41

I
Ireland, 59
Italian, 110

J
Jackie Gleason, 81
Jackie Gleason, 67

K
Krispy, 34
L
Lasagna, 25
Lemon, 56
Little Cesar, 101,114
Lombardi, Gennaro, 33
M
Maker's Mark, 68
Marshmallow, 82
Marvin gaye, 81
Mashed potatoes, 38
Meatloaf, 68
Meringue, 114
Mousse, 83
N
Navy Beans, 39
Nevin, Ira, 34
New England, 54
New York, 76
O
Oliver Twist, 60
Olives, 57
Onion, 65
P
Pancakes, 88
Parker House Hotel, 81
Parmesan, 48
Peaches, 119
Pepe, Frank, 33
Pero, Anthony, 33
Pie, 79,99,107,114
Pistachio, 96
Pizza, 35
Pizza Hut, 34
Pork, 29

Potato, 32,37
Pudding, 84,120-121
Puff pastry, 113
R
Raspberries, 76
Rib Eye, 46
Rice, 120
Rolls, 89
Russet potatoes, 32,62,65
S
S'more, 82
Sasso, John, 33
Sausage, 50
Scotland, 59
Sour cream, 57,67,74,76-77,103,104
Steak, 44,46
Sweet, 81
Swiss, 96,97
T
Tart, 107-108
Tempering, 70
Tenderloin, 46
Tiramisu, 117
Toast, 86
Truss, 70
U
United Kingdom, 59,121
V
Vanilla, 74
W
Waffles, 23
Wales, 59
Y
Yeast, dry, 35

www.ingramcontent.com/pod-product-compliance
Lightning Source LLC
Chambersburg PA
CBHW041218240426
43661CB00012B/1078